# IN PRAISE OF SHAME

... shamed persons are incapable of processing information, for a shame attack is like being drunk.... information on how to facilitate the process of shame so that transformation takes place makes this a valuable book which deserves a place on therapists', social workers', and counselors' shelves.

*Diane Fassel, Ph.D.*
*Author of* Working Ourselves to Death  and Adult Children of Divorce
*Co-author of* The Addictive Organization

---

...yet another example of the Mind/Body connection-how our thoughts and feelings directly affect our health. ...very thorough research...important and necessary book.

*Ruth Stricker,*
*Founder /Director of the Marsh: a Center for Fitness and Balance*
*National leader on mind/body connections*

---

We live in a culture that for generations has collectively and individually used shaming behavior to control its members. ... Yet shaming is always devastating to health and creativity. ...unresolved shame is at the core of many illnesses and causes needless human suffering.

*Christiane Northrup, M.D.*
*Assistant Clinical Professor of Obstetrics and Gynecology, University of Vermont College of Medicine*
*Author of* Women's Bodies, Women's Wisdom
*Past president of American Holistic Medical Association*

...for many people going through a divorce or custody dispute, shame is at the core of their problems and pain. I wholeheartedly recommend this book.

*Susan Lach, Attorney*
*President of Family Law Division of American Trial Lawyers*

---

...wonderfully healing perspective...eloquently uses quantum physics and a holographic view...to illustrate the power of shame.

*Anthony L. Sutton*
*Author* Breaking Chains: Hope for Adult Children of Recovering Slaves

---

# SHAME:
*Spiritual Suicide*

# SHAME:
## *Spiritual Suicide*

By: Vicki Underland-Rosow, Ph.D.

Waterford Publications
Shorewood, Minnesota

**Shame: Spiritual Suicide**
**By Vicki Underland-Rosow,Ph.D.**
**Waterford Publications**

The Twelve Steps reprinted with permission of Alcoholics
Anonymous World Services, Inc.
Excerpts from *Beyond Therapy, Beyond Science* used by permission of Anne Wilson Schaef.

Cover by Jennifer Velline

FIRST EDITION

Cataloging-in-Publication Data

**Underland-Rosow, Vicki**
 **Shame: Spiritual Suicide.**
 Bibliography: page 127
 Includes index
 1. Shame.                        2. Addiction.
 3. Psychotherapy-Alternative treatment.
 4. Spirituality              5. Emotions
 6. Mental health             7. Self-help
 8. Suicide

BF575.S45 U48 1995        152.443        94-090834
ISBN 0-9644944-2-6

## DEDICATION

I dedicate this book to my family;
my parents Virginia and Arthur Underland,
my grandparents Clarence and Leonore Walsh,
my life partner Ric Rosow,
and my children Michael and Katherine.
Each offered strength,
encouragement and love to me.
Each of them have been heavy on support
and light on shame.

# TABLE OF CONTENTS

# FOREWORD
by Anne Wilson Schaef, Ph.D.

Writing about a new paradigm is never an easy task especially as it takes some time completely to shake the dust off our sandals and begin to walk in new ways. Dr. Underland-Rosow believes shame belongs within the old paradigm. We are becoming increasingly aware that trying to heal the ills of the old paradigm with techniques of that same paradigm only exacerbates the problem and, indeed, often more firmly entrenches the very disease we hope to heal.

Shame is one of the interesting processes of the Addictive System. We tend to think of shame as a feeling and, as Underland-Rosow points out, it is not. Shame is a learned response that evokes a pseudo-emotion.

As I once heard a woman say at an intensive; "Shame isn't a feeling. I learned shame. Shame was used to control me as a child, and I took it in, and now I use it for control. Whenever I do not want to hear something I go in to my shame and nothing gets in."

In an addictive system, shame is used like a drug. People who go into shame attacks (described by Underland-Rosow) behave like drunks. I have long observed that there is an interesting relationship between shame and confusion. Both are learned responses. We are not born confused. We learn confusion just as we learn shame. Once we have learned shame and confusion and taken them into our being, we can call them up on demand as a way of not dealing with ourselves or our environment. There is an additional "goodie" to be gained from going into a shame or confusion attack. That "goodie" is adrenaline and it can be used as a very effective drug. We carry it with us at all times, and it is easily "self-injected." High doses of adrenaline result in a "drunkenness" similar to an alcohol high. When we are drunk, no information gets in. Nothing clear gets out. We have the illusion of controlling our environment, the way we have felt controlled.

To see shame as systemic and integrated into the culture is yet another important leap. We have not finished with this shame business; Underland-Rosow gives us a springboard.

*Anne Wilson Schaef, Ph.D.*
*Author of* Beyond Therapy, Beyond Science
Women's Reality
Codependency : Misunderstood/Mistreated
Meditations for Women Who Do Too Much

# ACKNOWLEDGEMENTS

*Shame: Spiritual Suicide* is about the effects of shame on people's lives and on their spirits. The experiences described are those revealed to me by people with whom I have worked. Names and some identifying details have been changed, and occasionally composites have been used to protect the individuals involved. I want to thank them for sharing their experiences of shame with me and permitting me to share them with you.

The concepts of the Living Process System, Living in Process and deep process facilitation expressed in this work were developed by Anne Wilson Schaef, Ph.D., over a period of several years as an alternative to traditional psychotherapy and as a way of healing that is congruent with a holographic paradigm. (In brief, the holographic paradigm sees everything as connected to everything else. This concept will be explored in detail later in this book.) These concepts are the subject of two books by Schaef, *Beyond Therapy, Beyond Science* and, now in preparation, *Living in Process*. Schaef has graciously given me permission to use portions of the unpublished material in this book.

I have been using the Living in Process approach in my consulting practice as a Living in Process facilitator for the past eleven years. My understanding of the concepts has evolved and grown as I have used them myself and witnessed the responses—and transformations—of people to whom I have introduced them.

Many people have traveled with me on the journey that writing this book has been. My Ph.D. committee at the Union Institute—Drs. Michael Patton, Elizabeth Minnich, Diane Fassel, Anne Wilson Schaef, Linda Moore, and Christie Randolph—all assisted me in countless ways. Anne Wilson Schaef, especially, has been my friend, mentor, critic, and inspiration. The entire Velline family has supported this endeavor: Karen, my partner and friend, provided countless hours of support and encouragement, her husband Bob and sons, Jeff, Tom, and Rob provided the title, and daughter Jennifer designed the cover. Others who have been instrumental in supporting and challenging my ideas include, but are certainly not limited to: friends and colleagues Alice Young, Barbara DeCosse, and Cathy Montgomery; and the many Process Network trainees, participants, and group members who contributed immeasurably to this work. Thanks to both Silvia Rosen and Beth Milligan for their editorial assistance. And a special thanks to my family—Ric, Michael, and Katherine—for their ever-present encouragement, love and support.

Shame is an unacknowledged national epidemic that is wreaking havoc on our entire society. Until it is acknowledged, challenged, and treated, we will continue to experience spiritual suicide on a massive scale.

*Shame: Spiritual Suicide* exposes the hidden costs of the shame experience. Virtually everyone in our culture has experienced shame at one time or another. Many of us, however, experience shame as a formidable underlying force ready to rear its head without warning. Shame results in disconnection: from self, from others, from the universe, from a Higher Power. When experienced on a regular basis, this disconnection leads to spiritual suicide, the death of the spirit.

Spiritual suicide can be recognized once we know what to look for. On an individual basis, spiritual suicide manifests itself through profound hopelessness. People who are spiritually dead often choose to live on the edge, always pushing the limits of danger, abusing themselves and others, vainly searching for meaning only to be consistently disappointed. Non-recovering addicts of any kind are classic examples of spiritual suicide. On a larger scale, group or societal spiritual suicide can be seen in the way we treat our planet and its resources. Pollution, crime, epidemic drug and alcohol abuse, discrimination, institutional sexual harassment are all examples of a society moving into spiritual suicide. Physical destruction and eventual death is the logical progression following spiritual suicide. People, both individuals and groups, who are no longer connected to their spirits cannot remain functional on this planet.

Shame by its nature demands secrecy and diversions. *Shame: Spiritual Suicide* breaks down the barrier of silence and shows how shame can be transformed, how a person or group can reconnect and again become spiritually whole.

*Shame: Spiritual Suicide* challenges the commonly accepted attitudes regarding the role of shame in creating a "controlled" society. The planet is on the verge of a new way of experiencing the world. Quantum physics is teaching us that disconnection and the illusion of control are not part of a natural environment. This work looks at many disciplines: quantum physics, the new science of chaos, psychology, medicine, religion, education, and economics to point out the development of a new paradigm in which shame has no function or value.

In a country plagued with rampant suicide, especially among our very young and very old, we would be wise to consider the connection between *Shame: Spiritual Suicide* and the act of physical suicide.

# SHAME:
## *Spiritual Suicide*

# Why Shame And Why Me

Many books have been written about shame. Why another one?

The common wisdom about shame is that it is necessary, that there is "good" shame and "bad" shame, and that a certain amount of "good" shame is essential to human moral and social development. As a practitioner of the Living in Process approach developed by Anne Wilson Schaef, I vehemently disagree! Shame is neither good nor necessary, but it *is* integral to an addictive culture which promotes disconnection, dishonesty, and judgmental attitudes toward people and behaviors. It is only by confronting that addictive culture and the way we operate within it that we can *transform* shame, and in the process, transform ourselves.

I first realized I had something different to say about shame when I was speaking to a large audience of therapists. I do not remember the actual topic of my talk, but what I do remember is the audience response when I said, *"It is foolish to expect a person experiencing shame to remember anything said to him or her. Talking to a person experiencing shame is like talking to a drunk."* Everyone in the audience suddenly reached for paper and pencil to write down what I had said. I was stunned. I thought that anyone who had ever been witness to a shame episode surely must have come to the same conclusion. The reaction to my simple observation, however, awakened me to the fact that many therapists do not recognize the fact that *people are unable to process new information while they are experiencing shame.*

My entire adult professional life has been spent working with others who, like myself, were searching for meaning and happiness in their lives. I often encountered people who were fairly successful by all outside appearances, but inwardly were the *"walking dead,"* people without spirit. For many years, I did not have a name for this phenomenon; I was too busy making psychological diagnoses. But finally, in the midst of a personal crisis of my own, I came face to face with the realization that my many years of training as a social worker and psychotherapist were not helping anyone, including me. I came to see myself as part of the problem. Thus began an odyssey into a new way of being in the world, a new way of interacting with myself and others.

## The Experience Of Shame In My Own Life

During the early stages of my own recovery from depression after the birth of my second child, I experienced a profound experience of shame, an experience that irrevocably changed my understanding of the role of shame in our personal and group evolution on this planet.

While shame had never been one of my "issues," when clients spoke to me of their shame, of *being* ashamed, the words of course were familiar to me and I assumed I knew what they meant. So I was astounded by the way I was affected, the way I *felt* when a seemingly minor incident at the mental health center where I worked *shamed* me.

One day, during a staff meeting, the chair of the department accused a group of his staff (including me) of billing clients for missed appointments, a practice which he believed to be unethical. He was verbally abusive, and threatened to fire anyone who did not "shape up" immediately. I responded by defending our actions and clearly stated my view of the situation. To my surprise and dismay, no one else in the meeting said a word, although afterward people came to me privately to congratulate me for standing up for my principles. I left the meeting angry at the chair, and hurt and disappointed that my colleagues had remained speechless throughout this interchange.

Later, I was suddenly and unexpectedly overpowered by shame. I seemed to fall into an abyss, a black hole, that was unlike anything I had ever experienced. This episode lasted for about twelve hours. During that period I was unable to concentrate on or to communicate what I was feeling to anyone. I seemed to be totally separated from myself and from what I believed. I began doubting my own therapeutic and ethical abilities, even though what I and others within the department had done was standard practice in many counseling centers and even though no client had ever made a complaint to the clinic about this practice. Then the self questioning suddenly turned ugly; I moved from questioning the particulars of what I had done to questioning my very core worth. I began to fear that my friends and family would disown me because of this issue. I felt desperate, unlike anything I had ever experienced before.

Yet when I finally was able to tell a colleague how I was feeling: that I was questioning my own ethical and therapeutic abilities because of the remarks the chair had made the day before, the shame ended. Her response was like someone throwing cold water on me and shocking me back into reality. She threw her head back, laughed uproariously and almost screamed at me, *"You are the most ethical and honest person in this entire place. You are being crazy!"* With that I immediately felt myself return to normal thinking. I soon joined her in laughter and before long we were on to another topic. Breaking the isolation by telling someone else, then feeling support and acceptance from my colleague, helped me to reconnect with myself and with what I believed.

After thinking about this episode for a long time, I came to see it as a gift. It was my "aha!" moment. For years I had worked with people immobilized by shame. *But, without even realizing it, I had never really under-*

*stood it.* After experiencing the blind-sided shock of debilitating shame firsthand, however, I began to understand just how profoundly incapacitating it can be. The event that caused the shame has faded into insignificance for me, but the *experience* of shame is one I'll never forget.

The episode also helped me see how closely the behaviors induced by shame resemble those of addiction. Addiction occurs when compulsive abuse of substances (e.g., alcohol, drugs, food, cigarettes) or processes (e.g., work, sex, relationships) separates the addicted persons from their feelings, from other people, and from the sense of social belonging. So, too, people experiencing shame find themselves isolated from their feelings and from other people. Addicts cannot concentrate or communicate. They are able to focus only on their addictions. In the same way, shame renders people unable to concentrate and unable to communicate meaningfully. They can focus on nothing but their shame.

### Living in Process

I don't believe in coincidences, and it was surely no coincidence that my deepened understanding of shame occurred at the same time I was learning and beginning to embrace the Living in Process principles developed by Anne Wilson Schaef. I have found in my work in the intervening years that the most meaningful antidote to shame is the conscious application of these Living in Process concepts, combined with active participation in a 12-Step program or group.

Briefly, Living in Process is a way of being in the world, of participating in one's own life, with others, with nature, and with a Higher Power. Using any means to distort, deny, or avoid one's own feelings is antithetical to Living in Process. Schaef believes that Living in Process is the natural way that human beings connect with each other, and that our distortions are a result of rejecting who we are and of unconnecting from the universe and others in it.

Believing as I do that shame is a "dis-ease of disconnection," Living in Process is a way to, stated most simply, reconnect and stay connected. The Living in Process concepts—and how you can apply them to your own life and your own experience of shame—are discussed in detail in the final chapter of this book, "Recovery and Healing."

### Transforming Shame

People living with shame have the ability to transform that shame if they are willing to participate in a great paradox. Only by experiencing shame and accepting, rather than denying it, will a person or group move out of it and into a life not dominated by shame. The way we deal with shame within an addictive culture reinforces shame and encourages its growth.

When we talk and listen and work with others who are accepting their shame and openly dealing with it, we can let shame open doors to feelings long dismissed, powers long denied, and an acceptance of self unlike anything we've ever known before.

Miracles happen when spirits return to hollow human shells. The people whose stories are told in this book are living proof of the miracles which have occurred in their spirits and their lives. With their shame acknowledged and transformed, they now experience life in a way they previously did not know was possible. Others can follow in their path. But it does involve taking a "leap of faith" into unknown and greatly feared territory, into the realm of the spirit, and a world of acceptance of self previously unallowable.

# EXPLANATION OF TERMS

There are a number of words used throughout this book which may be unfamiliar, or to which I refer with a very particularized meaning in the context of healing from shame. They are as follows:

**Shame** A feeling of inadequacy at the core of the self. Shame is felt for being a mistake.

**Guilt** A feeling that is evoked by a specific behavior that is deemed wrong or unacceptable. Guilt is felt for making a mistake.

**Addiction** Any process or substance used compulsively to avoid, distort, deny or enhance naturally occurring feelings.

**Disassociation** A form of isolation in which a person so disconnects from an experience, an event, or a part of the self, that he/she consciously denies its existence or importance.

**Reductionism** The reduction of things and ideas into their component parts to achieve control, a key feature of the scientific method since Newton.

**Holographic paradigm** A paradigm (or model) in which the whole is enfolded into all of its parts.

**Mechanistic World View** Belief that the world is a machine that can be taken apart and put back together again.

**Living in Process** A theory of healing developed by Anne Wilson Schaef as an alternative to psychotherapy, rooted in the 12-Step model of mutual help and healing.

The Living in Process philosophy is based on the premise that traditional therapies mirror an addictive system which is actually part of the problems most people enter therapy to overcome. Central to this philosophy is the belief that we are all inherently interrelated, and that without external controls imposed upon us, we have the capability to live at one with our selves, each other, and nature. It is distinguished from therapy by its active de-emphasis on control, interpretation, and manipulation. Most Living in Process facilitation (it is not called therapy) occurs in groups with one or more facilitators (who are not called therapists).

**Deep process** A term coined by Anne Wilson Schaef for the re-experiencing of old feelings, memories, and visions that are stored in the body but are usually unavailable to the conscious or "rational" mind.

**Intensive** A three to nine day Living in Process group session in which participants live, work, and heal together in a retreat setting.

# CHAPTER 1
## SHAME IN AN ADDICTIVE SOCIETY

We live in a society that is terrified of feelings. In the addictive system that characterizes our culture, feelings are avoided through the institutionalization of shame and the use of the addictive process. Both are diversions. Both are taught and supported by external forces. Each feeds upon and reinforces the other. Alternatively, shame is used to avoid facing an addiction and then the addiction is used to avoid facing the shame. Both are used to distort, deny, or divert feared and unwanted feelings. The use of the addiction as a "fix" to avoid experiencing shame is a temporary solution; it merely results in compounding the problem by increasing the shame. And so the cycle continues.

Acceptance of shame as a useful technique is based upon the acceptance of systemic addiction in our society. Anne Wilson Schaef exposed our entire society as an addictive organism in her book, *When Society Becomes an Addict.* She describes an addictive society as one in which social problems are denied, the majority of the population are not able to achieve personal fulfillment, individual lack of success is regarded as a personal flaw, the importance of feelings is denied, and unsuccessful people are shamed. All of society operates within the addictive paradigm and holographically the components mirror each other as well as the larger system and its relations with other societies and the universe. This results in individuals, families, organizations and the entire society all operating addictively. Shame is necessary within an addictive system.

This is what one woman, who came to see me initially about anxiety attacks, had to say about the way she experienced shame: "When I experience shame I feel as though I am looking at the world through shattered glass. Nothing is clear. I cannot hear anything that is said. Colors blur. My mind goes blank. All my attention is riveted on hiding my deficiency. It seems as if everyone can see right through me—and can see that I am inadequate as a human being. At that point, all I know is that I must hide. I must divert everyone's attention from my inadequacy. Sometimes I disassociate so as not to feel. Sometimes I lash out in a 'rage attack' as a diversion. It has devastated my self-esteem."

Many of the people I have worked with during the past 20 years were plagued with shame. None came with the express purpose of dealing with shame but as we worked together shame often surfaced. I learned how to recognize and name it. The more I learned about shame the more I saw it as very different from feelings such as hate, love, anger, fear, happiness, or joy. It has a bigger presence in one's life than these feelings. It takes over. It operates like an addiction. Addiction is any process over which we are powerless. Then I began to see that shame supports addiction and addiction supports the experience of shame.

## The Two Major Flaws
## In Traditional Approaches To Shame

In reviewing what others have written about shame, I came upon the work of Helen Lynd, whose book, *Shame and the Search for Identity,* was published in 1958. In it, she briefly describes how shame is holographic. Every other serious work on shame written in the United States since 1958 quotes Lynd, but none seems to understand or to follow up on her ideas regarding the relationship of shame to the holographic universe. None, until Anthony Sutton in *Breaking Chains*, makes the leap from the focus on the individual or family to the more inclusive systemic focus.   None questions the legitimacy of using shame as a control tactic.   Therein lie what I believe are *the two major flaws in most theories about—and treatment of—shame.*

*1.    Shame is accepted as a necessary element in a society that wishes to control its population.* This idea is based on the philosophical belief that children and adults need outside forces to regulate their actions. Studies on shame have usually focused on the difference between "healthy, necessary" shame and "unhealthy, debilitating" shame. These studies do not question the legitimacy of the cultural belief that social control of the individual and the use of shame as a control are necessary.  I find the acceptance and use of shame as a necessary component to control society to be rooted in the addictive paradigm.   In this paradigm, which was described by Anne Wilson Schaef, all of Western society operates addictively.   That is, our culture is founded on a hierarchical, control-driven world view in which the primary principle is that humans must be molded away from their natural instincts. This molding away from natural instincts occurs through disassociation.

What is not commonly recognized is that the act of disassociation is abusive.  This is equally  true at the individual, family or system level.  We can see that disassociation on the individual level often leads to not

27

knowing what is good for you and what is harmful. Disassociation can be seen in blackouts, accidents, addictive behaviors, and other dysfunctional behavior. Dissociation from the larger system means disconnection from nature and the world at large. When individuals and groups are disconnected from nature and themselves, they are incapable of discerning what is good for the system. This lack of discernment has fed, among other things, into the plunder and rape of the environment in most industrial societies.

**2.** During the past 10 years, the connection between shame and addiction has been firmly established. *What has not been recognized is the connection between systemic addiction and systemic shame.* This is a serious flaw in most psychological thinking because it leads to focusing only on individual and family shame which is, at best, a band-aid approach to dealing with shame. Systemic shame must be examined if recovery is to occur.

My review of the material written about shame disturbed me enough to stimulate my own research into shame as a personal and cultural phenomenon. I began by not only analyzing what it has meant in my own life but, also documenting the shame experiences of the people I worked with in my private practice and the participants in the workshops I conducted over the course of three years. The following is one woman's story:

Marlene was a 35-year-old, single woman when I first met her. A major theme in her life was disconnection and isolation from her body, her feelings, and her spirituality, as well as from other people and from a Higher Power. She was terrified of her feelings and would do anything to avoid them. This was the reason she gave for isolating herself; she was terrified of letting anyone get to know her for fear they would become contaminated by her.

We met when Marlene, a student, attended a class I was teaching at a college. Our first conversation took place after class in which I assigned the writing of a paper. She asked for help: she did not understand how to carry out the assignment. What did I want her to say? I said I wanted her view of her life and of why she had chosen to become a social worker. "I don't know how to do that," she answered.

Several weeks later she handed in the completed assignment. She was visibly distressed as she did so and she pleaded with me not to release the information it contained to the college administration. When I read the paper I could not understand her fear. The paper contained no incriminating information. Yet the same thing happened with each subsequent assigned paper. Later, she told me that for each assignment she had written two papers: one that was truthful and one that she thought would be "acceptable." Each time she struggled over which one to hand in.

Six months after the course ended Marlene called me at my consulting office. She wanted to make an appointment to see me but not right away, she said perhaps several months in the future. I found the tone of her voice and her confusion about what she wanted very disturbing so I offered her my next opening. She accepted.

On the appointed day and hour, Marlene arrived for the first session. She was a 35-year-old, white, single, diabetic, female weighing over 300 pounds. At the time she also was suffering from pneumonia and cracked ribs but insisted, repeatedly, "I'm fine. I can handle it." She was unsteady on her feet. (When we left the office, I was unwilling to walk in front of her going down stairs for fear she might fall on me.)

During the first of our many sessions she was distraught and disorganized. She talked almost nonstop about abuse. I could not tell if the abuse had occurred in the past or was in the present. I could not tell if she was the perpetrator, the victim, or both. She alternately paced the room or huddled in a corner behind a sofa where I could not see her. Furthermore, she was easily distracted. My questions seemed to divert her attention so much that she could not answer them.

At the end of the hour I had many more questions than answers. Marlene was so disconnected from herself that she had no idea of what she wanted or what she believed. She could not even tell me why she sought consultation with me.

Beginning with our second session, Marlene brought a tape recorder and taped everything we said. At home, she transcribed the entire tapes. She used each transcription to make up questions to "test my honesty." The testing went on for many months. An unexpected benefit of the taping for Marlene was that in transcribing our sessions she was forced to listen to what she had said. Due to being so disconnected from herself, she could not remember the contents of our sessions so most of the information on the tapes seemed to be new to her.

Disconnection was a way of life for Marlene. She used disassociation, denial, terror, lying, judgmentalism and isolation in order to avoid the feelings that threatened to overwhelm her. Marlene had been physically, emotionally, and sexually abused by her father starting when she was an infant. No one stopped him. Her brothers and sisters also were abused and they too were helpless. Unable to remove herself physically from the abuse, she disconnected emotionally from her body. By the time she was 11 years of age, older family members were providing her with drugs on a regular basis. This drug abuse furthered her disconnection. She lived a shadow existence for the next 24 years. Her emotional disconnection became dominant as her drug, food, and other addictions progressed. Her life was driven by shame and addiction.

Marlene's disconnection manifested itself in many ways: the inability to remember what she had said; completely isolating herself from all adults; chronic and severe self-abuse in many forms: overeating, drug usage, self-medication, overworking, and living under unsafe and unsanitary conditions. Occasionally during our sessions together, she was so disoriented she did not know where she was or who she was.

She was out of touch with her feelings to such an extent that she did not know how she felt about anything. She accepted physical pain as a normal condition customary for everyone. She isolated herself socially. She worked at three jobs (one was a physically demanding position at a facility for disturbed children) to support herself, her mother and her mother's menagerie of pets. They were regularly evicted from their apartments because the animals overran the property.

Marlene was a relationship anorexic, that is, she avoided relationships at any cost. A driving force behind this avoidance as well as her addictions was shame. The addictions kept her from being overwhelmed by shame. To escape experiencing shame, she would use and do anything to avoid all feeling, and especially to avoid looking at her life honestly. Her greatest fear was that if she did honestly face herself she would find "no one there." She saw herself only as her addiction.

By the time she began seeing me, Marlene was close to death. She was so out of touch with her body that she was unaware of her severe medical problems. She would begin coughing uncontrollably, but when I would inquire how she was feeling, she would say, "I'm fine, I can handle it." She was terrified of having a physical, so I met her at a doctor's office for her first physical in 15 years. After she filled out the medical questionnaire, I asked to see it. She had lied throughout. When I asked why, she seemed stunned. Lying was so much a part of her life, she literally thought nothing of it.

Marlene was afraid to tell the doctor the truth about her medical condition. Lying was preferable to the possibility of experiencing shame. Even when telling the truth might spare her physical harm, it seemed more important to her to avoid shame. Even a misdiagnosis seemed preferable to telling the doctor the truth about her medical history and experiencing shame.

About six months after I began working with Marlene, I invited her to attend a weekend intensive, a group in which about a dozen women participated at a retreat center. She considered herself to be so poisonous socially that she was sure her presence would ruin the entire weekend for everyone else and that my partner would never work with me again.

When Marlene came to the weekend intensive she began her long road to recovery. The first step was merely to connect with other adults. She spent the first 24 hours not talking to anyone, sitting outside the group with her back to the wall. For two full days she listened to other women tell their life stories. Suddenly, standing against the wall next to a door, Marlene began talking, and she talked nonstop for over an hour. Then she bolted out the door and disappeared into the woods. This was a huge step in her dealing with shame. For the first time outside our individual sessions she let other people hear part of her story and see her pain. The experience was life-giving for her. Although she had years of recovery work ahead, she had begun connecting, with herself and with others.

Marlene began facing her shame by telling part of her story; first to me, then at the intensive, and at the ongoing weekly group she joined later. Much of her life was unavailable to her conscious memory because she had disassociated herself when much of the abuse had occurred. Because some of the abuse had started before she was verbal, she could not put words to it now. She gained access to these memories, however, through deep process work. She needed to witness other members of her group doing deep process work for a long time before she gave herself permission to experience her own feelings enough to go through a deep process.

With each deep process, and with each telling of a part of her story, Marlene began to reconnect with more and more of herself. She no longer fears that there is "no one there" when she thinks of herself.

Marlene went through treatment for her drug addiction and has been in recovery from that addiction for more than ten years. After one year of sobriety with drugs, she quit smoking. As the years have progressed she is facing one addiction after another on her road to recovery.

As Marlene faced her addiction and began to re-experience feelings—any feelings, she began to do "deep process" work. "Deep process" is the term coined by Schaef for feeling and re-experiencing old feelings, memories, visions, etc., that are stored in the body but usually are unavailable to the individual through rational thought processes. When a child experiences something before he/she is verbal, the child "remembers" it on a feeling and visual level but has no words for it. The body remembers, even when the mind cannot. The same is true for the person who experiences something traumatic and deals with it through disassociation. The person's body experiences the trauma, even when the mind disassociates. Therefore, the body still has the experience stored within it. Deep process allows the body to tap into experiences that are not available to the conscious mind. The individual doing deep process work gains access to information that is repressed from the conscious mind but is still available if the individual is willing to participate totally in her or his deep process.

Marlene's deep process work allowed her to remember and reconnect and begin healing from her childhood trauma. She began to experience the return of her spirit.

Infants and small children do deep process work naturally. Unfortunately, this work is not valued in our culture; indeed, it is judged wrong and, therefore, children are systematically taught not to experience their deep feelings. When a child begins to experience strong feelings, the parent often diverts the child's attention through food, threats, withdrawal of affection, or physical and/or verbal abuse. The child's options are to acquiesce to the parents' wishes, thereby giving up what he wants, or suffering the loss of parental acceptance and approval (i.e. love).

By the time most children grow up, we have become disconnected from our feelings. Most adults in our culture are terrified of strong feelings. It means "losing control" — and in our society that is a fate worse than death for many people. It was terrifying for Marlene to allow herself the freedom to do deep process work because of her belief that feelings were not allowed. Only through facing this terror did she begin to heal.

# CHAPTER 2

# SHAME: WHAT IS IT?

---

*Pudorem habere servitus quodammado est.*
*To feel shame is a sort of slavery.*
-Publius Syrus, 43 B.C.

---

## The Historical and Philosophical
## Base of Shame

Shame is used to control people. It begins in the cradle and continues for many people until death. Most religious leaders, philosophers and psychotherapists have accepted shame as a legitimate social tool to achieve compliance of people. My work as first a clinical social worker and then as a Living in Process facilitator has shown me that this premise is incorrect.

I believe that development of shame began with "disenchantment." According to Morris Berman in his book, *Coming to Our Senses*, disenchantment involves a disconnection, a separation into observer and object (that which is observed). Disenchantment means a lack of participation in one's own life and surroundings. Berman hypothesizes that gradual disenchantment began some 4000 years ago (2000 BC) and culminated with the rise of Newtonian science. He believes that pre-Newton, we lived in an enchanted world, *"a world of Hermetic wisdom where real knowledge involved the union of the subject and the object in a psychic-emotional identification with images rather than a purely intellectual identification.."* It is my contention that this gradual disenchantment was a major factor in the development of the shame experience.

I propose that with disenchantment came the belief in the need for an outside force to guarantee conformity and compliance. This force, embedded throughout our society, is shame. Shame occurs in the presence of disenchantment and is deemed necessary when humans experience disenchantment. When there is no division, no disenchantment, the possibility of feeling defective to the core is virtually eliminated. If a person is one with the universe, he or she cannot conceive of himself/herself as defective. If people live in partnership, at one with one another, the need to control is not an issue; therefore, shame serves no purpose.

According to Riane Eisler in her book, *The Chalice and the Blade*, when Indo-European and Semitic nomads invaded the Neolithic cultures of what is now central Europe some 4000 years ago, they controlled the people they conquered through enforced conformity and subordination. The invaders used physical and emotional punishment, the rewriting of myths, and the destruction of sacred spiritual artifacts and places to transform "partnership" societies into "dominator" societies. One technique was to judge as defective people who did not conform to the "dominator" model. The act of judging people as defective resulted in shame for those being judged. Shame was the means to accomplish conformity, a way to ensure specific kinds of behavior. Shame's major function has been to control human behavior. In the partnership model, control of humans was not an issue; it is the dominator model that needs such control.

Both Eisler and Berman have pointed out that the Judeo-Christian tradition wrought a God demanding singular allegiance. Priests became powerful leaders who educated their "flock" to follow the laws of the "only true" God. This systematic elimination of all options for communal, natural theology corresponded with the development of a male-dominated, violent, hierarchical society. As this hierarchical society became dominant, questioning the rationale behind a priest's behavior was not allowed; therefore, use of shame as a control measure was not questioned, but came to be regarded as normal human behavior.

The Judeo-Christian Bible separates the human species from nature. A literal separation between humans and the earth occurred when Adam and Eve were expelled from the Garden of Eden. Two basic concepts engendered by the story of the Garden of Eden have been central to Western culture's worldview: first, that shame is essential to control the behaviors of humans; and second, that adherence to Judeo-Christian beliefs guarantees their followers mastery over the universe.

According to Berman and Eisler, one way Hebrew rabbis increased their dominance and power was to declare "participation consciousness" a sin. (Earlier, Plato had declared participation consciousness an affront to the intellect.)

Participation consciousness involved direct contact with God. Even saying His name aloud was not allowed. Contact with God had to be through an intermediary, the rabbi or priest. This systematic separation of humans from God served to further our disconnection from ourselves and our universe. This disconnection, when exposed and judged, is shame.

Norbert Elias in *The History of Manners* shows the "advancing threshold of shame" from medieval to modern Europe. Elias saw the development of shame connected to the changing social mores regarding daily life (eating, table manners, burping, etc.). These changing social mores were brought about by a shift in how decisions were made as people became more self-conscious and more concerned about how they appeared to others. Therefore, social rules became more important. These rules served to distance people from their surroundings.

There are cultures which do not experience shame—cultures based upon connection to self, to others, to a Higher Power, and to the universe. Judeo-Christians have taken it upon themselves to "correct" these people — to teach them shame, to save them from themselves. The people of Hawaii are a classic example of a culture without shame in which, after contact with Christian missionaries, the ability to experience shame developed.

A more recent example is discussed in *Ancient Futures* by anthropologist Helen Norberg-Hodge. She chronicles the cultural changes in Ladakh, a small section of the Tibetan region of the Himalayas. Virtually untouched by Western society as recently as 16 years ago, the Ladakhs were a people deeply connected to themselves, their communities, the land, other living creatures, and a Higher Power. People were happy—so happy that, in studying them, Norberg-Hodge was sure they must be hiding something behind their ever-present smiles. Only after the introduction of Western culture—and its emphasis on technology and advancement—did this change.

As they experienced the breakdown of connections inherent in their acceptance of the natural order of the universe, the Ladakh people began to experience a disconnection from them*selves* as well. And with this disconnection, they learned to experience shame.

Native Americans report a similar experience. Before

they had contact with the "white man," shame was not prominent in their lives. With their forced disconnection—from the land, from their spirituality, from each other—Native Americans began to experience shame.

In *Breaking Chains: Hope for Adult Children of Recovering Slaves* Anthony Sutton names "slave-shame" as a dominant force in both the lives of descendants of slaves as well as in the rest of the population of the United States. Sutton shows how 400 years of slave-shame mentality have resulted in an entire group of people who are bound by shame, complemented by another group that reinforces the slave-shame.

## Questioning as a Tool for Shame

Alexandre Koyre, a great historian of science, defined "experimental interrogation," as a new form of communication with nature. It began as a tool of modern science during the seventeenth century. Science began doing controlled experiments, part of these experiments involved questioning of subjects being studied. Experimental interrogation disallowed mere observation. It demanded superimposing a specific structure in which to gather scientific knowledge. Experimental interrogation was not interested in empirical connections between phenomena but, rather, focused on interaction between theoretical concepts and observations. This new form of communication with nature removed man from direct contact with nature, while putting a theoretical concept between the human self and nature. This process was mirrored by what was happening in religion.

Interrogation became the standard vehicle for disenchantment or disconnection from direct experience with nature. Interrogation has spread into non-scientific communication; Western society is so accustomed to endless questions that many of us have come to regard asking questions as the polite and proper way to get to know another. Questioning is, in fact, seen as invasive by many non-Western cultures, Native American culture among them.

The invasiveness of interrogation can be seen in its most blatant form in a stereotypical "conversation" between parent and teenager; the teenager feels the invasiveness of interrogation and the parent feels the frustration of asking questions and not establishing any real connection with the teenager. The disconnection inherent in this type of interchange is obvious when looked at within this context.

Interrogation in Western cultures begins long before the teenage years when the parent, through endless questions, puts a barrier (in most cases, quite unwittingly, I believe) between her or himself and the child. Questions often serve as a means of extracting data which the other may not divulge if not asked. Children are quick to learn that questions may signal the beginning of a shame experience if the parent is unhappy with the answers provided. As a protection, some children learn to lie, avoid, or manipulate so as not to be caught by their parents' disapproval. For some, this process continues throughout life with the individual or group doing whatever is deemed necessary not to expose whatever might be disapproved.

I propose that this questioning, this interrogation serves as a barrier to true communication and to a feeling of connectedness with self and others. This pattern of interrogation has filtered down from science, into interpersonal communication and finally into communication with God. Many people in our culture appear to be unable to communicate with others or with God without questioning.

Politics and economics have often worked hand in hand to control individuals and groups through shame. The Puritans of colonial times used coventry, public stocks, and public hangings to set economic and social constraints. *The Scarlet Letter* by Nathaniel Hawthorne is a classic example of public shaming to insure specific behavior from citizens of the community. More recent public shaming occurred on a systemic basis during the McCarthy era of the 1950's. In an effort to control people's political opinions, public hearings were held in Washington ostensibly to eliminate communists from any position of power. These hearings are often referred to as modern day "witch-hunts."

Childrearing practices contribute to the development of shame. Our culture is built in large part on the English Common Law in which children were the property of the parents. The reduction of humans to the status of property is important in the development of childrearing practices. This belief, combined with the belief that children, especially very young children, were literally too young to remember what happened to them, set the stage for treatment of children that often borders on criminal but, until recently, was seldom seen as such. Within this mind-set, most children are exposed to a culture that does not value them for who they are and for what they are, but instead continually tries to coax, manipulate, or force them into what adults around them want them to be. This systemic non-acceptance of children is the beginning of individual shame and is a holographic mirror of the larger systemic shame of the addictive system operating throughout our society.

Religious, scientific, educational, medical, political and economic developments since the Middle Ages have contributed immensely to a reductionistic, mechanistic worldview. The main goal of this worldview is control.

One by-product of the goal of control is shame. As the western world became more reductionist, the use of shame as a control tactic became more prevalent. Few have questioned the legitimacy of using shame as a method of control.

However shame is defined, it has been used in our culture for hundreds of years by families, churches, and schools to "socialize" children and, in religious, business, educational, political, and social organizations, to control the behaviors (and even thoughts) of adults.

## Fear of Exposure

Helen Lynd wrote in *On Shame and the Search for Identity* that shame is experienced by an individual or group as sudden, unexpected and unwanted *exposure* to others of feelings that one is defective to the core of one's being; the feelings may be so strong the individual may be certain they are obvious to everyone and cannot be rectified. The sense of being defective, of profound inadequacy, is initially inflicted by outside forces. This feeling of profound inadequacy is compounded by the fear that one will be abandoned when others fully recognize the inadequacy. This experience of shame-induced inadequacy becomes the center of one's thoughts and feelings. The person or group believes that everyone is aware of and focusing on the inadequacy. Thus, inadequacies are magnified until they appear to *be* the person or group. The urge to hide, to protect oneself from more exposure of the inadequacy arising from the shame experience drowns out all else. It becomes so all-consuming, it takes over the senses. This results in the inability to take in new information. Lynn, a woman I worked with, suffered especially in this way.

Lynn was originally sent to see me by a psychiatrist, who was frustrated with his inability to treat successfully Lynn's profound depression. In addition to depression, Lynn's life was filled with terror—the kind of terror that leads to blackouts, denial, and paralysis. Lynn lived in constant terror that if people really got to know her they would find her disgusting. She devoted an extraordinary amount of time and effort to controlling other people's impressions of her by being "nice," considerate, and giving. She sent flowers or a gift to someone almost daily.

Denial featured prominently in Lynn's life. She was

adamant about how wonderful her family was. She saw her parents as "perfect" and herself as "worthless scum." It was only after more than a year of slowly piecing together parts of her life that she began to recall glimmers of the abuse she had endured from her parents. She had been the victim of sexual and emotional abuse as a child. She disconnected from this abuse so consistently that she had no memories of it when we first began working together. Yet she lived in constant terror, without knowing why. She regularly had long periods of blackouts during which she did not know who or where she was. She kept her name pasted on her desk at work so she could answer the phone with "Hello, this is Lynn Doe's phone. May I take a message?" Later, when she remembered who she was, she would return the phone call.

Lynn occasionally experienced blackouts during group sessions. When this happened, she did not know who she was, who we were, or why she was in the midst of this group of women. To cope, Lynn tried to become invisible. She shrank down in her chair, became very still, and stopped talking. She actually *looked* smaller. After they had witnessed this "transformation" a few times, many of the other group members could recognize when Lynn was in one of these blackouts. Someone in the group would calmly tell Lynn what was happening. We told her who she was, who we were, and what we were doing together.

Lynn judged everything she did. She could not take in a simple observation without judging it. When a new group member told her that she had a lot of energy when she talked, her response was to ask if that was good or bad. She saw herself as a poor friend, although her friends thought otherwise. She spent tremendous energy trying to prove to herself that she was a good friend but, in her own eyes, always failed. On the rare occasions when she inadvertently said something to offend, she would beat herself up emotionally for weeks. Lynn's disassociation, combined with her judgmentalism, exemplifies the essence of shame.

### Definitions of Shame

In *Shame: The Power of Caring*, Gershen Kaufman clarified the magnitude of shame in his definition that shame is *"...the affect of indignity, of defeat, of transgression, of inferiority, and of alienation....Shame is felt as an inner torment, a sickness of the soul."* Furthermore, he regarded judgmental attitudes as a vital component of shame:

> *...Shame originates interpersonally, primarily in significant relationships, but later can become internalized so that the self is able to activate shame without an inducing interpersonal event. Interpersonally [judgmentally] induced shame develops into internally induced shame.*

The feeling of being defective, part of Lynd's definition, is echoed in the experiential definition offered by Merle Fossum and Marilyn Mason, family therapists, in their book, *Facing Shame:*

> *...Shame is an inner sense of being completely diminished or insufficient as a person. It is the self judging the self....A pervasive sense of shame is the ongoing premise that one is fundamentally bad, inadequate, defective, unworthy, or not fully valid as a human being.*

Elizabeth, a brilliant, professional woman who first came to see me some years ago, experienced all criticism as life-threatening. She feared she would be abandoned if she wasn't perfect. She felt shame as a fainting sensation when she received criticism—whether actual, implied or imagined. In a cruel trick of the psyche, she also experienced a fainting sensation when she was praised (the reverse of criticism).

As a young graduate student, Elizabeth lived for a year in Italy. Each day when she went out into the street, she heard Italian men calling out to her, *"Madonna!"* Secretly, Elizabeth wished they would call her something more sexy, as she sometimes heard them call other young American women. One day when she was dressed in an outfit more flamboyant than she usually wore, she was greeted on the street with *"Bella Bambola"* (beautiful doll). Instead of feeling proud or flattered, she felt herself engulfed by feelings of shame and fear. She became so disoriented, she walked off the curb and crashed into the side of a bus. The force of the collision knocked her to the ground. She quickly got to her feet and boarded the bus, oblivious of its destination. She didn't care. Overwhelmed with shame, she only knew she needed to escape, to hide.

She spent her young adult years trying to conceal who she was. She married a man who needed the spotlight, so attention was usually focused on him. She went on to become an alcoholic, isolating herself from others more and more. She rarely left the house. Only after treatment for her alcoholism, and then participation in 12-Step groups and Living in Process work, did Elizabeth become more visible. When I first met her, she wore monochromatic clothes, usually all beige. She blended into the background. She now wears a wide range of clothes and often stands out because of her colorful outfits. More important, she no longer sits in the background in conversations. She is an active participant in the activities she joins. She recently agreed to do a one-person art show, where anyone who wants to can come and see her work. Invisibility is gone.

## The Difference Between Shame and Guilt

Shame and guilt are not synonymous. Guilt stems from one's own behavior (e.g. cheating on an examination; robbing one's employer), whereas shame becomes part of one's identity (e.g., the feeling that one is defective). Although the terms often are used interchangeably, it is important to distinguish between the two. Shame develops earlier than guilt. Shame involves the entire fabric of the person. It sustains the person's basic feeling of inadequacy at the core of the self. Guilt, however, is evoked by a specific behavior that is deemed wrong or unacceptable. Guilt is felt for *making a mistake*. Shame is felt for *being a mistake*. Guilt allows for retribution and atonement, shame does not. Recovery from guilt can be dealt with more incrementally, that is bit by bit. Recovery from shame requires an entire system shift or spiritual transformation. Helen Lynd said in *On Shame and the Search for Identity:*

> *Guilt, or self-reproach, is based on internalization of values, notably parental values—in contrast to shame, which is based upon disapproval coming from outside, from other persons.*

Merle Fossum and Marilyn Mason stated the distinction somewhat differently and more succinctly in *Facing Shame:*

> *While guilt is a painful feeling of regret and responsibility for one's actions, shame is a painful feeling about oneself as a person. The possibility for repair seems foreclosed to the shameful person because shame is a matter of identity, not a behavioral infraction.*

In their work, *Shame and Guilt: A Psychoanalytic and Cultural Study,* G. Piers & M. B. Singer also saw a difference between shame and guilt. They defined shame as the failure to reach goals and guilt as the transgression of rules, that is:

shame = failure       guilt = transgression.

Despite what appears to be a simplistic differentiation, they went on to show the effects of shame: that ultimately, the shame-based individual fears and expects abandonment and "death by emotional starvation." This "death by emotional starvation" may be seen most graphically in infants who are deprived of mothering and close attachments; they do not thrive. It can also be observed in people who have lost their ability to be alive. They are still eating and breathing, but it is obvious that any real spark of life is missing. I have had the opportunity to work with many such individuals in my practice. One was John.

During a baseball game when John was eight years old, he struck out at bat three times in a row. His teammates all had gotten at least one hit. As a result, John felt defective and ashamed. He never participated in organized sports again. For years, he sat in his front yard pulling out crab grass while the other boys on the team ran by on their way to games. He hated those boys and the men they became. Even now, he tenses up when he sees them. His wife says she can feel the hairs on the back of his neck begin to stand up as they drive toward John's hometown. Through recovery, he is just beginning to see how his resentments limit him.

John saw the baseball incident as the beginning of his isolation. He spent the next three decades alone, guarding himself from exposing any deficiencies. He had no friends and did not date young women.

Fearful of disapproval, John tried to make himself invisible. The fear limited him to behaviors and opinions that he believed would not draw attention to himself. He avoided pursuing his goals and aspirations, or ever trying anything new, because he was afraid that others might laugh at him or call him stupid. As a freshman in college he realized that other students held opinions which they expressed. John had none. An opinion would make him visible. This lack of opinions actually triggered more shame, yet he remained terrified of developing opinions.

John was plagued with the need for perfection. If he was not right, he felt worthless; so being right took on huge importance. Because he was terrified of trying anything new, his job was a source of great stress because he worked in a rapidly changing technological field. He was often in great conflict with his supervisor, in part because John was so defensive and in part because of his open hostility whenever he feared the exposure of any inadequacy. John reported, "Any mistake became monumental. Shame would overwhelm me. I would feel like I was under a microscope with everyone intently looking at what was wrong with me. I tried to hide—and when that didn't work, I attacked the person who brought up the mistake."

For John, shame was so powerful that he experienced life—at least portions of life—as "the walking dead." He enjoyed nothing. He never laughed. He could only allow depression, anger and rage to surface. John said, "When shame takes over, my first response is fear and paralysis. I can feel something that must be adrenaline shoot through my body and then I can't move well or think clearly."

Crucial to the healing of shame is the breaking of the individual's isolation. John remembered, "It took a long time for me to even be able to speak in a 12-Step meeting. I realized I was supposed to share my truth at the meetings but I couldn't, and I had immense shame about this fear of sharing. The meetings gave me the opportunity to sit with and feel my shame."

Only after he began recovery through Sex Addicts Anonymous did he begin to open up to others and to develop friendships with other people. In his work in a

Living in Process group, he has gone against all his childhood training. He now shares his feelings with both men and women. He is letting others into his life. Indeed, he is beginning to *live* his life. His spirit has returned. For many years he existed, but did not live fully. He was too busy warding off possible criticism to enjoy life.

After some time in a Living in Process group, John was able to see that his shame didn't begin at bat as an eight year old, but began much earlier. His father was an alcoholic and his mother a raving codependent. His mother expected John to fill in for her alcoholic husband, a job too big for a small boy. So John was continually faced with his inadequacy: he could not fix the family no matter what he did.

He developed a victim-perpetrator cycle, which is common among people experiencing shame. He lashed out at anyone who dared to imply he ever made a mistake. He became very rigid in his habits and expected others to comply to his standards. When things did not go as he planned at work he would explode. When I intervened on his workaholic behavior, he was on a self-destructive path that would have almost certainly resulted in his being fired. Instead, he chose to go to treatment.

The first year after treatment, John experienced many difficult times at work, but he discovered that when he genuinely connected with his co-workers, he was able to stop feeling that everyone was against him. His defensiveness decreased and his willingness to consider—and put into practice—new ways of thinking, feeling, and *being* increased. About 18 months after treatment, John was named the most valuable employee of the month! He had come a long way from his near firing.

John saw shame as a major motivator in his life. He saw himself cycling between addictive behavior and shame. In the past, when he experienced shame, he buried the feeling in one of his addictions (sex, food, or work). This usually worked to take the focus off the shame for a while. However, after a period of addictive "acting out," he would experience increased shame about his out-of-control, addictive behavior, which simply added to his underlying feelings of inadequacy and worthlessness. The cycle was endless.

Now, in recovery, John is able to short-circuit the cycle by reconnecting with other people, with his Higher Power, and with his own feelings. He is learning not to isolate or disassociate himself and become judgmental when he experiences shame.

As John recovers, he is much less likely to automatically respond defensively or to take everything that happens so personally. He has come to see that gossiping and complaining *about* others, rather than talking directly *to* them, amounts to a "slip" in his recovery. He is working diligently to find new ways of directly connecting with people at home and at work.

John has discovered joy and laughter for the first time in his life. He has a spark in his eye and a connection to his spirit.

### The Difference Between Shame and Embarrassment

Shame is different from embarrassment. What elicits embarrassment in one individual may trigger shame in another. Much is determined by the perception of the individual involved. Embarrassment involves a personal self-consciousness about a particular trait or behavior but does not involve the basic worth of the individual. Shame goes far beyond a particular trait of behavior; it exposes a perceived basic inadequacy of the person or group.

Individuals brought up in households where mistakes are accepted as part of life tend to experience embarrassment and/or guilt much more often than shame when they make mistakes.

## "Healthy" Shame: A Contradiction of Terms

Otto Allen Will stated that *"shame is a way of embracing cultural prescriptions of desired and undesired behavior."* My research has shown that shame does not serve this purpose, but, instead contributes to dysfunctional behavior, such as depression, isolation, disassociation, and rage.

Many writers seem to have accepted the belief that a certain amount of shame is necessary for the public good or shamelessness would occur. The basis of this belief is that humans are innately defective and need external constraints to keep them in line with the prevailing ethos. In *Shame: The Power of Caring*, Gershen Kaufman asserts that some shame is necessary. He sees the need for remedies only when shame-based individuals experience problems. Ron Potter-Efron agrees with Kaufman: *"It should be remembered that shame itself is not a problem,"* writes Potter-Efron in *Shame, Guilt and Alcoholism:. "It is an excess of shame, dominating an individual that distorts normal human development."*

Neither Kaufman nor Potter-Efron specify how much is *"some shame"* the quantity of shame that distorts development, or how the amount of shame heaped upon a person can be controlled. In our culture, police statistics indicate that many crimes are committed when the perpetrators are under the influence of alcohol or drugs. When the addiction is an outgrowth of shame, the latter is not a deterrent; instead, it may motivate people impulsively to commit dangerous and asocial acts of impulse, lust, and violence.

More recently, John Bradshaw, in his book, *Healing the Shame That Binds You*, defended "some" shame as follows:

> *In itself, shame is not bad....In fact it is necessary to have the feeling of shame if one is to be truly human. Shame is the emotion which*

*gives us permission to be human. Shame tells us of our limits. Shame keeps us in our human boundaries, letting us know we can and will make mistakes, and that we need help....Healthy shame is the psychological foundation of spirituality.*

I believe Bradshaw confuses spirituality and religion. Shame is the psychological foundation of many *religions*. Shame is antithetical to spirituality. Much institutional religion in our culture separates humans from themselves (their feelings, desires, and thoughts), from each other, the universe, and a Higher Power. Spirituality brings things together. Spirituality involves connections. Spirituality is often experienced as profound oneness with the universe.

Shame involves disconnection, separation, alienation. Spirituality has no need for disconnection: most Western religion demands separation and shame.

Bradshaw defines "healthy" shame as "the psychological ground of our humility" and "toxic" shame as developing when it "takes over one's identity;" that is, when it is internalized:

*To have shame as an identity is to believe that one's being is flawed, that one is defective as a human being. Once shame is transformed into an identity, it becomes toxic and dehumanizing.*

But shame, by its very nature, is *always* internalized—which means that all shame is "toxic" and there is no such thing as "healthy" shame! What Bradshaw seems to mean by "healthy shame" is humility. His difficulty in distinguishing between the two is evident in his defining "healthy shame" as the "psychological ground" for humility. More important, humility motivates people to change, whereas shame does not.

What Bradshaw refers to as a little shame—"healthy" shame—is actually the humbling of the spirit. But humbling does not involve the same dynamic as shame. Humbling means honest recognition of self. Shame doesn't allow for that connection, that recognition.

### The Difference Between Shame and Humility

In the philosophy of Thomas Aquinas, and in many recovery programs, humility is defined as the recognition that one has both strengths and weaknesses. It involves giving oneself credit when one has earned it and recognizing the credit one owes to others, especially a Higher Power. It requires the accurate perception and admission of ownership of a behavior or characteristic, a process that is not available to people who suffer from shame. Humility is what the fourth step of the 12-Step program (Alcoholics Anonymous and others) is all about. It reads, *"Made a searching and fearless moral inventory of ourselves."* The Al-Anon program expresses the idea as follows; *"Humility is honesty and depth of vision, a realistic assessment of ourselves and our part in the scheme of things. It places us in a true relationship with a Higher Power."* Realistic and fearless self-assessments are impossible when shame is present; thus shame is a hindrance to and entirely different from humility.

The experiences of Steve Jones, a Living in Process group participant, show the profound difference between shame and healthy humility:

Steve lived most of his life under the cloud of persistent, profound shame. As a child, he discovered that his worth was nothing. He was unacceptable to his father, and that meant he was unacceptable, period. Nothing he could do would change that. His only hope was to try to hide and become as numb as possible.

Steve grew up in a family where the job of the children was to make their father look good to the community. His father was the school superintendent in a small town where everyone knew the whole family. Mr. Jones did not allow Steve to develop his own opinions or beliefs. The rules were so stringent and all-encompassing that he and his siblings felt the watchful gaze of his father's "spies" everywhere they went. At a Boy Scout dinner, Steve left his tomatoes, a food he didn't like, on the side of his plate. The next day, he was punished for not eating the tomatoes. An adult at the dinner had called his father to report on what he did and did not eat!

When I first met Steve, he was in early recovery from drug addiction and alcoholism. In addition, he had recently completed a hospital stay duing which he received shock treatments. He was employed, but was terrified of having relationships at work or elsewhere. His only friends were left over from his drug-using days. As they were all still using, they offered no support for his recovery. His personal life revolved around avoiding his parents and caring for his dog. He experienced almost constant anxiety and would lie about anything rather than risk "exposure."

I do not advertise, so the people I work with normally come to me though the recommendations of friends or relatives. Steve is my one exception. I am listed in the Yellow Pages--just my name, nothing else. Steve picked me because he liked my name. So profound was his isolation, he had no one to ask for a referral.

After working with me individually for about six months, Steve agreed to join a Living in Process group. Through participation in this group, he gradually began to see that his childhood rules were not normal. One evening he put down on paper the scores of unwritten family rules imposed by his father:

> Do not talk
> Do not cry
> Do not laugh
> Do not succeed
> Do not fail

Do not have any opinions
Do not object
Be nice
Do not feel
Do not ask for help
Do not disagree
Do not swear
Do not play cards
Do not go on dates
Do not play
Never think of yourself
Do not frown
Do not get angry
You are not special
You have no rights
Do not say "No"
Do not act like a child
Punishments are severe
Do not be happy
Never say anything which may imply an achievement
Do not smile, except when with outsiders, then make sure you smile
Do not draw attention to yourself
Do not make any noise, especially during the day or when you go to bed
Dad gets food first—then eat as much as you can, as fast as you can, or you don't get any
Do not talk at meals
The TV must be on while eating
Do not try to change your role in the family
Dad can do whatever he wants, where and whenever he wants
You must beg if you want anything
You must never be honest and find ways to do things without telling Dad
If you look at the newspaper before Dad does, make sure you fold it to look like you didn't

before he gets home
Always have meat and potatoes for supper
Be on time even if you are running late
The house must be very clean for any
company
Do not let anyone know who you are
You will die if you don't do what you're sup-
posed to do
You must wear a bib when you eat
Never quit- no matter what the cost
You do not have a right to any privacy at any
time

Just as Steve finished reading the list to the group, there was a knock on the window. (A group member arriving late was locked out of the building.) Steve jumped clear out of his seat and screamed, *"It's my father!"* Even as a middle-aged man, Steve felt his father's presence and feared for his life. (His father lived in another state and didn't even know that Steve was in a group.)

As a child, Steve was cut off by his father's rules from any freedom to be himself, to know his feelings or opinions, to explore the world. He and his siblings lived with constant fear of what their father might do. An older sister introduced Steve to drugs and alcohol while he was in junior high. Steve had already developed a successful technique for becoming invisible in many situations and was able to graduate from high school without anyone confronting him on his drug usage. He constantly worked at being invisible. He never expressed an opinion. If no one saw him, he reasoned, no one would report his activities to his father.

He knew that trying to get help would be useless. On one occasion, his brother wrote a note to the counselor at school, pleading for help. The counselor took the note directly to Mr. Jones. After that incident, no one in his family attempted to get outside assistance for many years.

Steve came to see me because he was suffering from depression and shame. Both permeated his life. He was a walking shadow. He felt he had no soul. Spiritual suicide was nearly complete. He felt no connections. He was miserable and wanted something different, but because of his background he had little hope that something different was possible for him. People like Steve are amazing. Growing up in a family where connections were not allowed, they still attempt to establish a kind of human connection they're not even sure exists. Somewhere beyond consciousness is a drive toward health and wholeness that I find awe-inspiring, even after more than two decades of working with such people.

As Steve became an active participant in a Living in Process group, he began to little by little, expose what he felt were his terrible secrets. He began letting others see him, know him. He also joined a 12-Step group, something he had been loath to do for many years. In the 12 Step group he began to take his inventory, something that demands an honest appraisal of strengths and weaknesses. (Most people in 12-Step programs have more trouble making a lists of strengths). Through his participation in both these groups, Steve has discovered strengths he never knew he had. He no longer sees himself as a "blight on the face of the earth," but rather acknowledges that he has worth and is lovable. He has become an honest person. His opinion of himself is non-defensive, non-depreciating, and non-bragging. His description of himself appear based upon reality, not fantasy. He has discovered true humility.

Steve is transformed now. He has found his soul, he has found his voice, he has found his feelings, opinions, and beliefs. He is seeking a spirituality based upon connections, not on the religious pretensions of his father. He has developed friendships that are deep and honest with men and he is working on developing deep and honest relationships with women. He is an inspiration to other group members.

As part of his recovery, Steve has begun "giving back" to the larger community. On Thanksgiving and Christmas, Steve and a friend spend the mornings taking food to people who are home-bound. He recently began graduate school in social work. As he connects to previously disowned parts of himself, there is more of him available to connect with others. This connection begins a new cycle — formed through affiliation, not isolation.

### The Shame Paradox

Shame is paradoxical. While it forces the person or group to become self-centered, at the same time the person or group *loses* self — and spirit. As a result, the person or group becomes disconnected: from the self, from others, from the universe, and even from a Higher Power.

*Shame is not an inherent feeling like disappointment, fear, hurt, joy, or sadness. Rather, it is an experience, something that is imposed upon a person or group. It is, consequently, a constellation of feelings, behaviors and states of being.*

When in the midst of a shame episode, the individual or group feels isolation, fear, rage, depression, inadequacy, confusion and exposure. Simultaneously, the person or group feels the focus of unwanted attention as well as utter loneliness.

Initially, shame is imposed upon a child. A person or group forces the experience upon the child and teaches the child that it is shameful. Shame is learned, therefore, in the context of a relationship. It begins as an external pressure imposed upon the individual (or the group) to establish compliance.

### Yearning for Connection

It doesn't take long for a child to start imposing

shame on him or herself, without prompting from other people. What begins as an external control quickly becomes internalized if it is experienced often enough. Shame begins with disconnection between parent and child and the child's fear that he or she will be abandoned. In *Shame, The Power of Caring,* Kaufman talks of the break in the "interpersonal bond" during a shame experience. This break, this disconnection, occurs between individuals and, at the same time, within the individual as well. The child must disconnect from parts of the self to try to reconnect with the parent. This need to reconnect is the drive to regain parental approval, and it sets the stage for subsequent dependence upon others to form one's self-esteem and self-worth. Children who abandon the self to gain parental approval set the stage for the subsequent dependence upon others to determine self-esteem and self-worth. Reliance on others to validate or deny one's self-worth is a core component of the relationship addict.

The relationship addict is a person who, in attempting to be accepted by another, gives up himself/herself. The relationship addict will lie to avoid disagreement or conflict with another person, whether a close friend or mere acquaintance. The relationship addict often doesn't let herself/himself know what her/his opinions are as they might offend someone. In an addictive relationship one or both parties are disconnected from themselves, so their relationship cannot provide true intimacy or closeness. If one is not first intimate with oneself, one cannot be intimate with another. One is unable to risk honesty with another for fear of abandonment.

## Shame and Addiction

Shame and addiction are intertwined. One is inevitably followed by the other. An addiction, as Anne Wilson Schaef has described it, is any process or substance that an individual or group uses compulsively to avoid or distort naturally occurring feelings.

Alcoholism, drug abuse, workaholism, sex addiction, eating disorders, relationship addiction, and romance addiction are some manifestations.

In Webster's Dictionary, the root of the word addiction is given as *"addicere: to give oneself up."* Addiction, says Schaef, is any process over which we are powerless.

> *A sure sign of an addiction is the sudden need to deceive ourselves and others—to lie, deny, and cover up. An addiction is anything we feel **tempted** to lie about. An addiction is anything we are not **willing** to give up....*

A paradox of addiction is that it is something over which we have no power, but at the same time we are consumed with the illusion that we control it. The illusion that we are in control is the cornerstone of the addictive process. It is recognized in the first step of the 12-Step Program that states, *"We admitted we were powerless over alcohol, that our lives had become unmanageable."* This step must be taken before healing can begin.

Addiction and shame alternate with one another as diversions. Shame is a diversion from the feelings, wants, and desires which the child has been taught are unacceptable. So too is addiction a diversion from feelings, wants, and desires that are deemed unacceptable. The unacceptability of the feelings was usually determined by a parent when the child's behavior or failure to act did not meet parental approval.

### Childhood Shame

Many people report parental attempts to shame them ranging over the gamut of behaviors. One man remembers his shock when his mother unexpectedly verbally attacked him for singing in the back seat of their car. He had been happily enjoying himself in song when suddenly his behavior was unacceptable, for no reason he could fathom. He only knew he must stop what he was doing or risk further rage from her.

Children are often shamed for not maturing as quickly as a parent wishes them to. Children are shamed for using a pacifier, needing a comfort blanket, wanting hugs, being afraid of the dark, etc. The child using a pacifier may be told, "Either get rid of that thing or else!" The or else often translates into "I won't love you."

Children who are sexually abused are given a message that their bodies are not their own, but can be used by another. The child cannot physically leave, but he/she can emotionally disassociate from her/his body. This is the tactic many children take. As one participant of an intensive group session relayed, "My choices were few. I could leave my body and go and sit up on a shelf looking down at my father sexually abusing me, I could go mad, or I could try to stop him and probably be killed. I chose the shelf. Now I have trouble staying in my body whenever I get stressed."

The judgment does not always come from a parent, nor does the judgment need to be of a cruel intent. One young girl talked to me of her shame in being mistaken for a boy in a store. In relating the event to me a year later, she still had difficulty talking about it. She was affected tremendously by one off-handed comment from a woman she did not know. Since then, she has refused to cut her hair and has taken to wearing clothes that make her gender apparent.

When children experience parental withdrawal, they often feel fear of abandonment. The child learns to separate himself/herself from the feelings, wants, desires the parent finds objectionable. To a small child, the choices seem few: either abandon part of self (wants, feelings, desires, needs, etc.) or be abandoned by the parent. Both choices bring fears of abandonment, isolation, disassociation, and inadequacy. The first choice often means spiritual death; the second, physical death.

## The Systemic Nature of Shame

Lack of recognition of shame as a larger societal issue has kept the focus on individuals, perpetuating the individual's belief in individual inadequacy. Unless shame is seen in its larger arena much of the treatment of shame will continue to be of a "band-aid" type; it takes some of the sting out but does little to solve the underlying issue. Crucial in understanding shame is consideration of the holographic aspect of it.

Ignoring systemic shame forces on individuals more responsibility for personal shame and, at the same time, it disallows true recovery by permitting examination of only a portion of the problem. By focusing on individual shame and thereby repeating the process of separation that is the originator of shame, shame is dealt with in a reductionistic manner.

## Diversion and Disconnection

Shame, according to the renowned psychologist, Erik Erikson, in *Identity, Youth, and Crisis,* is a *learned* experience, a diversion taught to infants by their parents. It serves to distract, destroy, and deny the feelings deemed undesirable by parents or other caregivers of infants and small children. This diversion serves to control infants from trusting their own knowings: thoughts, feelings, perceptions, impressions, goals, etc. The diversion (shame) continues and becomes internalized so that many adults go through life without clear connection to what they actually feel; rather they experience shame whenever a "non-acceptable feeling" begins to emerge.

Disconnection appears to be inherent in the dominant Western culture. We are disconnected from each other, from nature, from a Higher Power and from our selves. Every time a parent tells a child to stop feeling a certain way the parent is ordering the child to disconnect from a part of itself.

When individuals or groups are disconnected, they are more easily manipulated and, at first glance appear to be more controllable. However, despite the common belief, shame does not control behaviors; rather, shame creates enormous dysfunction at all levels. What is generally overlooked is that shame debilitates. Let us examine further the dysfunction inherent in the shame experience.

## The Holographic Paradigm

The systemic nature of shame and addiction is seen within the framework of a holographic world view. According to quantum physicist David Bohm, who describes the universe as one living organism, the "holo-movement" involves the concept of "unbroken wholeness." Perhaps an example will help to clarify these admittedly complex concepts:

We are all familiar with holographic photography, the reflective, three-dimensional-looking images we often see printed in magazines and on credit cards. In traditional photography, the image is composed of hundreds of tiny dots. When a section of the image is magnified—of, for instance, the wing of a butterfly—what is visible is a blur of dots. The image cannot really be seen, piece by piece. It must be seen whole to be accurately perceived.

In contrast, when a portion of a holographic image is magnified, the *entire* image becomes visible. Each piece of the image contains within it the totality of that image.

To take the concept an order of magnitude further, picture the *entire* universe as actively enfolded into each of its parts. Because the whole is enfolded into each part, all the parts are therefore enfolded into all other parts. This means that there is profound internal relatedness, a concept which Bohm calls the "implicate order."

Shame is enfolded throughout our society. Our whole society is based upon the illusion of control.

Control is attempted through system-wide denial and devaluation of vast portions of our processes. Individuals and groups are coerced, cajoled, manipulated, and battered into disconnecting from their thoughts, feelings, and hunches, and from their connections with others.

Bohm states that *"The true state of affairs of the material world is wholeness. If we are fragmented, we must blame it on ourselves."* This fragmentation is part of modern science's attempt to control through reductionism (the act of reducing, separating things to their most elementary components). It can be seen in isolation, disassociation, denial, blackouts, and abandonment. Each of these acts is an attempt to fragment the self from others, a Higher Power, nature, and/or a part of self.

Exposure of fragmentation along with judgmentalism about the fragmentation is manifested in individuals and groups as shame. Shame is not inherent in nature. It was developed by and imposed on people, and people can transform shame by reconnecting to the "implicate order." Reconnecting to the implicate order means reconnecting to the holographic world of which we are naturally a part. Distress comes when we attempt to disconnect from that of which we are inherently a part.

Along with the discoveries in quantum physics, there developed the "new math," a geometry that focuses on systems as a whole. It places relationships and interconnectiveness at the forefront. Further, the new math mirrors holographically what is occurring in other disciplines: the vision of the world as a holograph. Thus, mathematics has joined physics to reveal a nonlinear world view.

In his book, *Chaos*, James Gleick tells us that traditional mathematics is predicated on the assumptions of reductionistic logic. Linear systems can be taken apart and then put back together. Non-linear systems cannot.

Linear differential equations could account for changes in which small changes produce small effects and changes in which a series of small changes produce proportionality larger effects. Linear equations could not, however, explain discontinuous things, such as sudden high winds or explosions. Mathematics could not explain much of natural phenomena until Lorenz found, with his Butterfly Effect, that while systems *almost* repeat themselves, they are never absolutely identical. The Butterfly Effect states that "*a butterfly stirring the air today in Peking can transform storm systems next month in New York.*"

Use of shame to control behaviors has been based upon a linear logic:

    A. a parent disapproves of the child behavior

    B. the parent responds with judgment and breaks the "interpersonal bond"

    C. the child ceases the undesired behavior.

Put mathematically, A+B=C. What we tend not to consider seriously are the nonlinear, fractal[1] aspects of this scenario. To examine those aspects means moving the focus to the entire system's movement. When this is done, we see that shame does not control just one particular behavior, but affects the *entire person*—and thus, holographically it affects the entire universe.

As described in mathematics, the shame experience can repeat itself for a period of time with seemingly stable results and then suddenly there can be a dramatic and unpredictable shift into a new behavior. The undesirable behavior may indeed cease, but at the same time give rise to a whole complex of new feelings and behaviors, e.g., rage, depression, inadequacy, isolation, fear, and anger.

Quantum physics, mathematics, and various other disciplines have joined forces to create a new evolving science, the science of Chaos. Chaos is bringing us to the brink, individually and collectively, of a new way of experiencing the world: an environment in which control is an illusion rather than a fact and open systems are constantly flowing and changing. Through developments in Chaos theory, people are coming to realize that any change they force upon another being, through shame or other means, may result, in a *"bifurcation point"* which they can neither predict nor control. With this knowledge comes a new view of the fallacy of using shame as a controlling measure.

Studying natural systems, one can observe repetitive movements and then, at some critical point, see a sudden new movement occur. An infant suddenly shifting from one type of activity into an entirely new one is an example of this. Transformation involves this process of repetitive behavior, chaos, and then a dramatic shift into new behavior. Recovery from shame mirrors this repetitive action. A sudden critical point (bifurcation) occurs with a period of chaos, followed by transformation of shame into a new behavior where shame is no longer operable.

The acceptance of holographic concepts transforms how we experience ourselves and how we participate in relationships with self, others, the world and a Higher Power. Acceptance of the holographic world view requires reconnection and participation. It also requires recognition that judgmentalism, the illusion of control, and the exclusive use of linear logic are no longer needed. In their place there is regained a oneness with self, others, the universe, and a Higher Power. This oneness is spirituality. Shame has no place in spirituality.

When shame is used as a controlling device, it is made part of the holographic universe. Individual shame, which isolates the individual does not occur in isolation. Individual shame is a holographic replication of systemic shame. It is a part of a larger systemic phenomenon embedded in Western reductionistic culture. Until this concept is recognized, we will continue to deal with shame under the old paradigm of the reductionistic, separatistic, logical, linear thinking of the Newtonian scientific method.

To treat shame adequately, its holographic aspect must be recognized. By ignoring systemic shame, individuals are forced to take all responsibility for their personal shame. At the same time, recovery is disallowed because only a portion of the problem is examined. Unfortunately, most therapists tend to deal with shame as if it is an individual flaw, and in so doing *separate* the individual from society, thereby repeating the fragmentation and isolation that is at the root of shame.

# CHAPTER 3

# HOW SHAME FUNCTIONS

Shame, we have seen, is used for many different purposes. Some parents use it to control a child's behaviors, that is, to make the behaviors conform to parental standards. In other words, they shame the child for being a child, for having the wants or needs appropriate to a child. Thus parents may shame a child for being afraid of the dark, for being shy with strangers, for wanting comfort from the parent, for singing too loudly, for crying after a fall, for confusing truth and imagination, and just for being alive and vibrant.

Some people use shame to protect themselves from public exposure as abusers. They are usually people in positions of power, such as parents, employers, or public or religious figures. Indeed, victims of harassment or abuse—whether sexual, physical, and/or emotional—often report that the perpetrators attempted to shame them into compliance and silence. Gary's experience exemplifies this:

Gary had been physically, sexually and emotionally abused for years as a child. He vividly remembers standing at the top of a flight of stairs when he was 11 years old and saying to himself, "What happens to me is not important. Anyone can do what they will with me because I don't matter anyway."

Gary had been told by his abusers, both his father and grandfather, that they abused him because he deserved it. Both father and grandfather blamed Gary for their sexual abuse of him. His father threatened him with banishment from the family if he ever told anyone what was happening. His grandfather told him that everyone would know that Gary was evil and therefore was the cause of the sexual abuse.

Like most abused children, Gary did not understand, at the time, what was happening to him. Beginning in his early teens, he took drugs and alcohol to, in effect, anesthetize himself. As he grew older and began to understand the enormity of what had happened to him, using alcohol and drugs became a way to bury his feelings of shame. The addictions became a way to keep shame at arms length. But he found that shame grows as addictions progress. A vicious cycle that began externally became internal as addiction and shame fed off one another.

Gary's relationships were based on shame. "I sought out people who were verbally abusive and I tried to get them to accept me so I could have self-worth. Shame actually provided an illusion of control in my relationships. I figured I wouldn't be abandoned by my friends because I used shame to control them."

Shame is a spiritual crisis; shamed individuals see no value in their place in this world, nor in the next. As Gary put it, "I am so awful that I contaminate anyone who comes near me, so I isolate myself. I reject God because I know that God would reject me." Shame had taken over. Gary perceived no way to reconnect with himself, others, God, or the universe.

In recovery from his addictions Gary was able, little by little over the course of several years, to begin *living in his body* again. He needed to relearn what feelings were like. Only after seeing others in the group experience their own feelings again and again over a two year period did he come to the realization that experiencing feelings was different from being crazy.

Gary's disconnection from his feelings had encouraged him to become passive and to be a victim on many occasions. As he began to experience his feelings, he found himself less of a victim.

For the first time in his life, Gary is dreaming dreams, not nightmares. In a recent dream he experienced what he interpreted as a spiritual connection. In the dream, a beautiful, wise, strong man offered to be his spiritual guide and Gary accepted the offer.

Recovery for Gary means reconnection. He sees the need for the connection with others and he is taking a leap of faith to attain it. Even though he is terrified that others will discover that he is inadequate, defective, and unlovable, he has become a valued and valuable group member, reaching out to others both during group sessions and in his free time outside of the group. Instead of isolating himself at work, as was his pattern, Gary has become an active participant in the social interactions within his office. More importantly, Gary is beginning to accept himself. He laughs more, occasionally makes spontaneous decisions (like going out for dinner without planning it weeks in advance), and is beginning to see some beauty in life. His spirit has returned.

## Denial, Disassociation, and Childhood Abuse

The victims of childhood abuse often buy into the compliance and silence by silencing themselves *to* themselves. They achieve this through disassociation, denial, and/or withdrawal into their own world. Many disassociate from the abuse enough to lose conscious memory of it.

When the silence is finally broken, often years or even decades later, the reactions of others may recreate the original feelings of abandonment, of not being believed, of being judged the troublemaker. Today, many women and men are speaking out publicly in greater numbers about early shame experiences, especially those involving sexual abuse. Some people who expose the harassment or abuse they experienced are accused of lying (e.g., Anita Hill) and are penalized or castigated for not speaking earlier.

One woman I worked with had such an experience. When, as a teenager, she finally told her family about the sexual abuse she had endured at the hands of several of her older brothers, her parents promptly had her declared insane and placed on the locked psychiatric ward of a hospital. There she was given massive doses of tranquilizers until she recanted her charges of abuse.

The underlying message of shame is "You are not good enough and nothing you do ever will make you good enough." Children of alcoholics often experience feelings of inadequacy, as if the family problem is their responsibility. At the same time, children of chronically ill parents, whether they are suffering from alcoholism or another disease, often are expected to be more capable than is developmentally possible, as the experience of Louise illustrates:

Louise remembered vividly when her mother became chronically ill. At the age of four, Louise, the oldest child, began to take over parenting responsibilities in the family. Louise always felt inadequate and, in truth, she was too immature to carry out the responsibilities thrust upon her. She grew up knowing that her place in life was to make sure that she never hurt anyone close to her. At age 15, when she broke up with a boyfriend, she was so distraught about hurting his feelings that she tried to commit suicide.

Louise spent thirty years trying to right the wrongs of the world. She worked with abused children and found that regardless of how competent and caring she was, most children  continued to live in  abusive situations. No matter how hard she tried, she could not change the entire system.

When she first joined one of my Living in Process groups, Louise was suicidal. She was living with her husband, a man she feared. She regularly drove her car at unsafe speeds. She  ignored exhaustion.  Indeed, she felt she had no right to be alive. She coped with  shame about her inadequacy by disconnecting from her body. She regularly  bumped into things, yet never knew how her many bruises occurred.

Louise spent a great deal of her life disconnected from everything, even herself. Whenever she became uncomfortable with something, her spirit, her essence, would leave her body. At such times, she actually looked blank, she would withdraw from the group into a place where no one could touch her. Others in the group might be laughing, or grieving, but Louise would sit there, utterly unengaged, like a piece of stone.

When she first attended a Living in Process group, Louise was not aware of this behavior. As we came to know her, we gently and without judgment called her attention to her disconnection when she "left." Gradually, Louise was able to know when her spirit was not in her body.

As she began spending more time "in" her body, Louise also began to reveal more and more of herself to the group. She had been very careful, initially, to tell only things she wanted us to know.  Eventually, she began letting others in the group see the parts of her that she felt were disgusting and unlovable. She also began spending time with some participants outside of group. This made it less possible to separate her life into compartments. At the same time, she began to eliminate people who were abusive from her life.

"Deep process" work helped Louise reconnect with her body and her feelings.  Allowing herself to experience feelings without judgment or fear of censure established a new pathway that enabled Louise to take in information. Memories long forgotten suddenly became available. Patterns emerged and missing pieces came into focus. Through this process, Louise has become more honest with herself, her family, her colleagues, and her friends.

Louise still experiences shame, but it no longer controls her life. She now sees shame as an invitation to accept her feelings, which is very different from her old way of living. Previously, shame was a command to divert, distort, and deny her feelings. It also forced her to comply with whatever demands were made on her.

She now sees shame as "a clue to me that I am in my disease, that I'm probably hiding something that I need to expose and speak out about."

Shame also often serves as a kind of self-protection for the child being victimized. Jane, the child of an alcoholic father stated, "I think, when I was a child, that experiencing shame was my way of making sense out of craziness. When in shame I would withdraw and be quiet. I think it also was a method of self-preservation. I believed that if I expressed my rage, I would be killed."

The function of shame changes as a child matures. Andrew, a recovering workaholic told me, "While I was trying to grow up, shame functioned to keep me obedient. It was a useful tool for the people who raised me to keep me from disclosing the secrets of their lives. Now, shame functions as a catalyst for my addictions. When I am aware of feeling shame, I feel very empty inside and I try to fill that emptiness with anything (food, sex, alcohol, drugs) that will induce a different feeling."

As shame becomes more and more dominant, it takes on other functions. Dick, a member of one of my groups, described the power of his experiences of shame. "The shame keeps me from living fully. It allows me to hold onto my addictions and keeps me from having to experience my real feelings. It reinforces my self-abusive behavior. It keeps me in a cycle of not feeling good about myself, self-abuse, and not feeling good again. It's my jailer."

Unwanted exposure of one's shame—even the fear of such exposure—is extraordinarily painful.  In an attempt to avoid the pain, the individual or group  often develops behaviors that are manifestations of spiritual crisis and dis-ease:  fear of abandonment, isolation, dis-association, blackouts, denial, terror, lying, judgmental-ism, paralysis, rage, self-centeredness, depression, and fear of criticism.

### Fear of Abandonment

Abandonment, according to Gershen Kaufman in *Shame: The Power of Caring*, is the primary fear of the shame experience. The child may experience a parent as suddenly, unexpectedly, and unexplainably  withdraw-ing violently from the child.  The reason for the with-drawal is sometimes never made clear to the child; what is clear, however, is the experience of shame and fear of abandonment.

Abandonment takes various forms.  The most obvi-ous is actual physical withdrawal.  Children with par-ents unable or unwilling to care for them are left on door steps, in alley ways and in churches.

A less obvious, less dramatic form of physical aban-donment occurs in our traditional, accepted forms of childrearing in this country.  Parents may leave a child unattended for short periods of time, believing the child is safe.  Parents going out to the store or taking a daily run may leave when the child is asleep, and the child wakes, cries, but receives no response.   Many parents do not understand the terror evoked in a child who finds himself/herself alone.

Children are often threatened with abandonment if they do not "measure up."  Statements such as "We will send you to an orphanage" or "Someday I will walk out of this house and you will never see me again" are common. Our society condones parents abandoning children after a divorce. It is not uncommon for the non-custodial parent (usually the father) to discontinue financial support of his children after the divorce, thereby financially abandoning the family. Government agencies generally turn a blind eye to this practice as if it were culturally acceptable.

Emotional abandonment is more common than physical abandonment. Our culture actually encourages emotional abandonment. Our culture is built on doing more, achieving recognition, and juggling family, work, and recreation. Workaholics are highly regarded. Workaholics, however, are emotionally unavailable to themselves, let alone to others, including their children.

The fear of abandonment often overshadows the internal abandonment that occurs. When shame is experienced, the person fears abandonment from the other and then, almost simultaneously, the person abandons herself/himself. This kind of abandonment is internal and can take many forms: psychologically leaving the body; denial of feelings; distortion of feelings; self-abuse to divert unwanted feelings, etc. Internal abandonment leads to many of the other processes involved in the shame experience. Internal abandonment begins the process of spiritual suicide.

Even our medical procedures surrounding childbirth contribute to the development of fear of abandonment. Joseph Chilton Pearce, author and lecturer, states that the first trauma that children in developed countries experience is during the very process of their birth in a hospital. Immediately after birth, the infant is suddenly and unexpectedly (at least to the infant) taken away from the mother and placed in isolation. This initial experience of abandonment sets the stage for later fears of abandonment.

At birth, the brain, as a hologram fragment, must have exposure to and interact with the earth hologram to achieve clarity, to bring the brain's picture into focus, so to speak. Separate a newborn from its parents and the ability to begin clarification is damaged.

Modern birth methods have been under attack from many sources for the past several decades. The result is a return to a more normal, natural birth process often without the attendance of a physician.

Our history books abandon entire segments of society by their systemic focus on some groups while ignoring others or portraying them in a negative light. Only as these groups begin to band together and to speak out are they able to change that practice.

## Isolation

*I don't want to belong to any club that will accept me as a member.* Groucho Marx

Isolation serves several purposes in the shame dynamic. First of all, infants who experience abandonment, experience feelings of isolation at the same time. Isolation is often used to control children's behaviors. The children are made to stand or sit in corners, placed in separate rooms, or in more extreme cases, tied to beds. They are left alone for long periods of time or even sent away from their parents. Mild forms of isolation (time outs; sitting in a chair; standing in a corner), are considered "good" forms of punishment because "no violence" is entailed. Yet anyone who watches small children's responses to these controls sees children express what is close to terror. In fact, these forms of isolation are shaming devices. Isolation at an early age encourages feelings of inadequacy because children know they cannot survive alone.

Isolation, a common form of punishment in prisons and other penal institutions, is used routinely to punish small children. Consider the comic strip, "Dennis," and his reactions to sitting in the corner, isolated from the rest of the world. When one woman related her first experience of shame she remembered sitting in her little rocking chair facing the corner, feeling very bad and ashamed. When she asked her mother about it, her mother said she had used the technique to toilet train her when she was around two years old.

Second, isolation may become a way of life. People fearful of exposure often use isolation regularly to avoid exposure. The isolation can be physical, emotional, spiritual, and/or psychological. One woman wrote: "I'm unable to go out to work. I feel unable to be in public. I'm so humiliated by my appearance. I isolate myself inside my house or drive around in my car and don't get out. I feel people will be poisoned if they have to look at me."

Internalized isolation is a haven and/or hell for the shamed person. Walls are erected to keep others from seeing the "true me." These walls take many forms. According to Anne Wilson Schaef, one way to isolate oneself without removing oneself physically is by "impression management." It allows a person to appear among people but to disguise himself/herself so as not to be vulnerable. The person attempts to present an image that he/she wants the world to see. Control is of paramount importance to the person who uses impression management to function in the world. Often this person appears to be "together" but more often he/she presents an impression of being aloof, arrogant, and distant. Isolation is often most acute when an individual is in a group but feels that he/she doesn't really belong in it.

Sleep is a common isolation technique. Many college students away from home and forced into communal living in a dormitory choose to sleep a lot as a way to isolate themselves from the group because they feel they don't belong.

Isolation also protects the individual or group from the scrutiny of anyone who may be able to see the internal flaw. In addition, isolation encourages obsessive self-examination. "I isolate my self from others in order to 'figure out' what I did or didn't do right. I obsess, ruminate, and block out the present. I feel ashamed, no good. I now hear clearly that accusing, still, small cunning voice inside me that says, 'You'll not measure up!'"

## Disassociation

Disassociation is common in the shame experience. Gershen Kaufman found that the shame-based person *"actively disown[s] parts of itself, thereby creating splits within the self."* Children have few alternatives when they are verbally, physically, or mentally attacked by parents. Most are incapable of physically removing themselves from the situation, thus they disassociate themselves. Disassociation is a basic element of shame. Shame occurs when a part of the self is disconnected from the whole self and this disconnection becomes apparent. Recognition of this disconnection often does not occur. Often people present at someone's shame episode are not aware that the act of disconnection is occurring in front of them. They may notice nothing or they may see the person suddenly appear shy, withdrawn, rageful and/or disoriented without recognizing the presence of the person's shame. Many times observers of the shame episode choose to ignore the shame, adding to the feeling of isolation and abandonment.

Disassociation is a particular form of isolation. In disassociation, the person so disconnects from an experience, an event, or a part of the self that he/she consciously denies its existence or at least its importance. Disassociation takes various forms:

1. Disassociation from the event through repression of the specific memory
2. Disassociation from entire portions of one's life in order to remove that time period from

         one's conscious memory

3.   Disassociation from specific parts of the self that are somehow connected to shame (sexuality, body, etc.)

4.   Disassociation from all feelings or from specific feelings

5.   Disassociation so profound that multiple personalities result.

For many people with whom I have worked during the past 20 years, significant periods of their lives were simply not available to their conscious memories. Some began their recovery with the awareness that something was not right with their interactions with the world, but are not aware of the cause of their discomfort. Often, these people were competent, capable, achievers by any external measurement. What the outside world didn't know is that these people were plagued with feelings of deep-seated inadequacy, regardless of their achievements. Others were just ordinary achievers, like most of the people we tend to know, and still others were marginal, people unable to function adequately in any segment of their lives.

These people began recovery because they were unhappy with their present lives and unable to remember much of their early lives. Often, our work together involved the gradual remembering of childhood events, many of which evoked long-repressed shame. The struggle that ensued, as the individual began to uncover long-buried shame, initially was often terrifying to the individual.

Incest victims frequently repress conscious memories of the incest but are plagued by unsatisfactory relationships and unhappy lives. Shame, recognized or unrecognized, often dominates much of their lives. For some of these people, an unexpected memory may occur when they are emotionally involved in something seemingly unrelated, such as watching a movie, listening to another person's story, engaging in therapy, or dreaming. If the person is ready to face the childhood trauma, he or she struggles with the memory rather than dismissing it, often at great short-term emotional cost. The years of training in disassociation are a formidable barrier, but the drive toward health forces many to continue along the painful path to uncovering long-forgotten trauma and the source of their shame.

### Blackouts

One component of shame may be a blackout. A blackout, according to Webster's Dictionary, is *"a momentary lapse of consciousness or vision; a loss of memory of an event or fact."* Blackouts occur because of disassociation of the self from an event. They are commonly thought of only in connection with abuse or with addiction to alcohol or drugs but, in fact, people addicted to *any* behavior are candidates for blackouts. Anne Wilson Schaef has observed that blackouts may occur when the person is physically present at an event but, because of an addiction (such as workaholism, sex addiction, food addiction, and many others) is not truly present. Nick, a member of one of my Living in Process groups, frequently experienced this kind of blackout.

Nick grew up with a father who was very opinionated and critical. His father took great pains to point out any mistake Nick or anyone else made. His mother, a classic relationship addict, allowed her husband to berate her and the children.

Nick was in his mid-thirties when I first met him. He often appeared to be scatter-brained or unaware of his surroundings. Family members did not believe him because he often did not follow through on the commitments he made. He would say something one day and deny ever saying it the next. He would promise to pick his daughter up after school and then forget to do so. When questioned about it, he would deny ever having agreed to pick her up. Blackouts allowed him to disassociate himself from events he found too painful or difficult to face consciously. What Nick's family did not understand was that Nick actually did *not* remember saying certain things if he was in a blackout at the time. Blackouts, like many of other behaviors inherent to the shame experience, feed into the development of even more shame.

A diversion Nick used to minimize his failure to follow through was lashing out at family members. At a recent workshop, he related that when he experienced shame he often diverted the experience by turning his rage on another, usually his son, or upon himself through self-abuse. Eventually, however, the feelings of shame returned, more overwhelming than ever, compounded by shame about his rage attack, and so the cycle continued. If Nick does not begin to break this shame-rage cycle, he will be at risk for more and more violent behavior.

To make matters worse, Nick has found a place to work that helps him recreate his shame/rage cycle. His department is in continual chaos as various employees verbally attack one another. The abuse is not exclusive to his department but exists company-wide. Recently, his company was successfully sued by several women for sexual harassment while on the job. The company's response was to become even more repressive toward all employees rather than to deal with the more basic issues. Individual employees are responding to the repressive rules by doing whatever they can to undercut the authority of the supervisors in every area. The work place has become a war zone. Nick is just beginning to see how his personal violence cycle is mirrored in his place of employment.

Blackouts are a very effective means of isolating oneself. It is curious that blackouts are rarely noticed by others. Once a person has begun recovery and has heard about blackouts, he/she begins to recognize the occurrence of blackout episodes in her/himself and in others. Almost everyone has noticed that sometimes a person may be so preoccupied that he/she has no idea what is being talked about. Yet few people recognize this behavior for what it is: a blackout, an abandonment of the present situation. Children are often more astute than adults at noticing when someone is not truly present.

Sometimes what may at first appear to be a lie actually may be the result of a blackout experience. For example, a person may "forget" to carry out a commitment and, when called to account, may adamantly deny having ever made the commitment. In fact, however, the person may have been in a blackout when the commitment was made.

### Denial

Writers Melody Beattie and Claudia Black have both shown that denial is basic to both addiction and shame. Many people who experience shame deny the experience, even to themselves. Denial is the act of disowning something or some fact. It involves a refusal to acknowledge to the self and/or others something one does not want to see. Denial takes many forms: blackouts or ignoring, distorting, or dismissing the importance of an event.

None of the people I work with initially presents shame as a reason for seeking help. When asked, many do not identify shame as a problem in their lives. Nevertheless, when they begin working on issues of self-abuse, addiction, and/or compulsive behavior, shame begins to surface. With the breakdown of denial, there often comes a period of intense feelings that include (but are not limited to) shame.

The experience of an acute shame episode is similar to being drunk. Information taken in by a drunk is distorted and often not remembered. Many times I have been called the day after a group member experienced a shame episode to be asked, "What happened yesterday?" Shame is an experience that prevents integration. The person becomes disconnected from the self and, therefore, the integration of the experience becomes impossible.

Schaef pointed out that denial may occur at a systemic as well as an individual level. Our country's refusal to acknowledge the crisis in our savings and loan institutions until bankruptcies occurred is a recent example of systemic denial. Many knowledgeable people warned NASA officials that the Challenger had unresolved problems and should not be launched, but NASA ignored these warnings and went ahead with the flight. Many other factors were involved in the decision to go ahead with the launch and denial was a contributing one. The result was the destruction of the space ship and the deaths of all aboard.

### Terror

The fear of abandonment, especially to a vulnerable child is equivalent to death. Terror is the natural result of such a fear. Terror is much more profound than fear or anger. It permeates every cell of the body, every part of the psyche. Terror is blinding. It can lead to blackouts, denial and paralysis. I have seen terror cause people to disassociate from an experience. Katie, an abuse victim, lived her life in constant terror without knowing why. She could never count on knowing who, or where, she was. When terror overtook her, she experienced blackouts. I once witnessed this happen to Katie with astonishing swiftness. We were together at a Living in Process "intensive" with a group of about ten other people. One afternoon, when Katie was playing a casual game of catch with two male friends, also participants in the intensive, one of the other players snapped at her impatiently in the heat of the game. Suddenly Katie didn't know where she was, *who* she was, or who the two men she was facing in this open field were. All she knew was that she was terrified and that it was not safe to let anyone know what she was experiencing. An hour or so later, after she had regained her memory and sense of reality, she shared her experience with the group. In Katie's life, this intense, consuming terror was the one dreaded constant.

## Lying

*"Lying,"* wrote Donald Nathanson in *The Many Faces of Shame*, *"is inherent in shame."* Shame often involves lying to one's self, lying through denial and distortion, and lying to the world overtly and covertly. Lying is almost always preferred to the possibility of experiencing shame.

Sometimes people lie without even knowing why or what actually has happened. Something from the past lets the individual know that the truth is not safe. This is what Jerome, a member of a Living in Process group, had to say about his first conscious experience with shame:

> *I was about 11, I guess, and had no idea of what an ejaculation was. I thought that I was bleeding and I ran into the bathroom (late at night) in a panic with my first 'nocturnal emission.' When my mother came and asked what was wrong, I lied and said 'Oh, nothing,' and I will never forget that lie. It was born out of complete ignorance, yet I felt compelled not to be truthful. I believe that I had already learned about shame, and that I was ashamed of what had happened, although I did not learn until long after what I had experienced.*

This boy, even in his panic about "bleeding," was unable to tell his mother the truth. The message was somehow clear: to let someone really know the truth was not safe.

## Judgmentalism

Judgmentalism is always involved in the shame experience. To be disapproved of, to be judged inadequate, is an underlying interaction of the shaming experience for children. This external judgment becomes internalized by children through repetition. With the internalization, the children then pass judgment upon themselves and others, thus continuing the cycle. There appears to be a direct correlation between the amount of judgmentalism and the amount of shame a person or group experiences.

Typically, judgmentalism involves dualistic thinking (good-bad, right-wrong). When something is judged bad, often the immediate knee-jerk reaction is "What can I do to fix it?" No time or energy is spent on exploring what the experience means; the person focuses instead on "How can I change or control it?" Thus, little learning occurs from the experience.

Children feel shame when a parent shows displeasure with what they have done. Many people, when questioned regarding their first conscious memory of shame, cannot remember what "shameful" thing they had done; what they remembered was the *reaction* of the parent.

Entire populations can be and are judged as inadequate, as less than. Present economic, political, and educational practices systemically reinforce judgmentalism toward such specific groups as Native Americans, Blacks, Latinos, Asian-Americans, women, disabled persons, and many others. This systemic judgmentalism fosters systemic shame for entire populations of individuals.

The purpose of social or systemic shame is to control individuals and groups. What people feel ashamed about is determined by the judgment of authority figures one loves and respects, the people or groups in power, and established custom. For example, the social response to early feminists in England and the United States who fought for women's rights was efforts to shame them; once the constitutional amendment was passed, however, the efforts halted, public opinion shifted, and politicians began to woo women's votes. Today, those early feminists are regarded as national heroes.

Public attitudes toward hair are another example of the societal use of shame as a control. Up until about the late 1960s, male students who let their hair grow beyond what was considered an acceptable length were derided publicly and suspended or expelled from school, a punishment designed to heap shame on them and their families. Attitudes changed, however, after the U.S. Supreme Court ruled in the students' favor, and today hairstyle is no longer a social issue.

## Paralysis

For some people, shame is so powerful that they experience life, at least for portions of their lives, as "the walking dead." Shame so overrules their emotions that they cannot permit themselves to feel anything other than depression, anger, and rage. Laughter, fun, and joy are missing from their lives, as are compassion, passion, and zest.

Because shame is so all-encompassing, shamed individuals are not able to take in new information during a shame experience. This can lead to paralysis—the inability to think, move, or speak.

Paralysis can occur even when the affected individual is doing rather mundane things. One woman I worked with stated, "My spouse had offered to buy me a handbag. We entered an expensive leather shop. I was immobilized almost immediately after being greeted by the sales person. I couldn't choose. I didn't feel I belonged there or had a right to purchase a bag, and I just spiraled down and down."

## Rage

Rage is commonly felt by many people or groups experiencing shame. Often it is used as a diversion, a means to distract focus from unwanted shame. Rage, like shame, overwhelms the senses. Like shame, it is all consuming. Rage is often spoken of as "blind." People feeling rage may not be aware of their surroundings or of what they are saying or doing. The rage drowns out everything except itself. New data cannot be taken in while either shame or rage is experienced. The same is not true for emotions such as love, anger, hate, pain, sadness, etc.

The violence of rage takes many forms. Individually, it manifests itself in self-abuse, abuse toward others, and abuse toward things (e.g., vandalism, littering, destroying our natural resources). Collectively it manifests itself in larger forms of self-abuse, such as a minority group rioting in their own neighborhoods after being shamed by people in positions of power.

I was once the victim of a co-worker's rage attack and only realized much later that her actions grew out of profound feelings of shame. This is what happened:

Three of us were involved in the meeting: Jim, Fran, and me. I was speaking with Jim when, suddenly, Fran interrupted and shouted at me, "You are really directing those comments at me. You don't think I did an adequate job!" I was stunned. I didn't know where that idea had come from and quickly said so. It was clear to me that Fran did not believe me when I told her my remarks were intended for Jim.

We went on to another topic. Fran made some point and I agreed with her. She turned on me and again shouted, "There you go restating my ideas and making me look dumb!" Again, I was stunned. Her comment made no sense to me. A little later in the meeting, I disagreed with her about something. Again she verbally attacked me, this time for disagreeing. Finally, she and Jim became involved in a discussion and I merely listened. Suddenly, Fran turned and accused me of taking Jim's side because I had been silent. At that point, it should have been clear that nothing I could do would be acceptable to this woman, but naively I asked her what she wanted from me. She told me she would like me to leave. I said, "OK," and gathered up my things. Just as I was walking out the door, she said, *"I can't believe you are leaving like this!"* Dumbfounded, I left the room.

Later, Jim told me that the experience had been eye-opening for him. He had been on the receiving end of many such outbursts from Fran, but they had been spread out over many months; mine were concentrated into a single two-hour meeting.

The next time we met, Fran shared some of her feelings of inadequacy and shame. That helped me put the attacks in perspective. I was the *recipient,* not the *cause* of Fran's attack of shame. Now, when I am faced with a person who verbally attacks me for something that doesn't make any sense, I consider that the person may be experiencing shame and attacking me as a diversion. I know that to talk to a person experiencing shame is like talking to a drunk, so I proceed accordingly. This means I do not take what the person says too seriously; rather, I check it out with the person another time. I also do not continue to engage in conversation with the person while he/she is acting in such a manner.

Rage is not limited to individuals. Entire groups—even entire countries—can become caught up in rage. Collectively, it can be seen on a multiple of scales, from gang activity to countries waging war.

## Self-Centeredness

Self-centeredness is a core component of shame. During the shame episode, the individual or group is so focused on hiding the perceived defect that everything else fades into the background. The person experiencing shame judges every event and circumstance from a totally self-centered point of view: "How does this affect *me* (and the shame I'm trying to hide)?" The person experiencing shame is sure that everyone is as obsessed as she or he is with the defect of personhood.

The person loses all sense of perspective, and only the defect stands out as important.

## Depression

According to Helen Lewis in *Shame, Guilt, and Neurosis, "Shame plays a central role in depression."* Many people with whom I have worked have experienced depression. One man described it like this: "I go into a black hole. Nothing can get me out of the depths of despair I feel when I am depressed. I can only see what is wrong with myself and the world. It seems as though nothing can elevate my defects. Everything is black."

As people work through their shame, the depression often lifts. Hopelessness is a component of depression: there appears to be no way out of the depression. Time seems to stand still. Concentration is difficult, sometimes impossible. Depression seems a logical consequence of feeling innately inferior and knowing that there is no way to fix one's defects.

I believe that depression, like shame, is a diversion away from feelings the depressed person is afraid to feel. The "feeling" of depression masks many other feelings. Once a person is willing to face the underlying feelings, both depression and shame dissipate.

The accumulation of all these isolating techniques is the loss of one's connection to one's essence. The mind/body/spirit connection is severed.

## Fear of Criticism

Fear of criticism keeps countless people from trying work they are interested in, and its crippling effects can even be felt by small children.

I once led a special reading group for first graders who were advanced readers. Kelly, the best reader in the group, always corrected any mistake I (or anyone else) made while reading. She, herself, never made a reading mistake. But when I asked the children to make up stories, she was stumped. She could not create a story, regardless of the topic.

Sometimes, I asked the children to create a story "by committee." Taking turns around the circle, each child added a sentence or two to the story. Most of them loved doing this. But not Kelly. "I don't have any ideas," she said.

I watched Kelly in other circumstances and felt great sadness for this child with a good mind who was afraid to create, to open herself to criticism, even when the group was non-critical.

New group members are often afraid to share their thoughts and experiences for fear of criticism. This fear is compounded when the individual, obsessing about what others may think, sets her or himself up to *expect* criticism, thus hearing as criticisms remarks which were not intended to be critical at all.

### Spiritual Crisis — and Spiritual Transformation

All of shame's manifestations — fear of abandonment, isolation, disassociation, blackouts, denial, terror, lying, judgmentalism, paralysis, rage, self-centeredness, depression, and fear of criticism — arise from a single cause: a dis-ease of the spirit. *Shame is a spiritual issue.* People who experience shame feel unworthy of life — either on earth *or* in heaven. As one group member once painfully put it: "I could find no God who would not reject me."

My work with shamed people highlights these doubts of a legitimate place in the universe. Shamed long enough, separated from significant others through emotional or physical abandonment and judgmentalism, the individual abandons the self and sees no place for the self. Spiritual suicide occurs. Disconnection is complete — from self, others, God, and the universe. Shame has taken over.

When I was first introduced to Mary she had been seeing a psychiatrist for years. She was on massive dosages of anti-depressants. She looked like a shadow person. Her spirit was missing. She was a shell. When I looked into her eyes I could see desperation, despair and immense pleading for help.

Raised in a fundamentalist religion, Mary found no consolation in God or a Higher Spirit. She grew up with an active alcoholic father and a depressed mother. A gifted artist, she was married to a highly successful professional and had three small children.

Mary was driven by shame. It permeated her every breath. She spent much of her time paralyzed. She obsessed for months about the proper clothes to purchase for her daughter's school wardrobe ( her daughter was in the first grade). She lived in terror of someone finding fault with her or her children. She was unable to form opinions for fear of being criticized, yet she spent most waking hours endlessly criticizing herself. She lived, no she barely existed, under constant siege from her own built-in judgmentalism. Nothing was ever good enough. She was never good enough.

Shame had so taken over that she ended her life. She told me that could not endure the pain, the isolation, the constant terror that was part of her very existence. She did not have the strength or will to honor these feelings or any other feelings. That left her with few options. Long before she ended her physical life Mary had disconnected from her spirit. Spiritual suicide was the precursor to her physical death. Mary was unable to find enough connections within this world to remain here.

Many recovering addicts see their addictions as a spiritual crisis. The same can be said for people experiencing shame. Spirituality is connection: to self, to others, to the universe, to a Higher Power. Shame breaks this connection and spirituality is damaged. When one is disconnected, one is often dispirited. With recovery from addiction and the transformation of shame, individuals and groups experience a profound connection to themselves, to others, to nature, to the cosmos, and to a

Higher Power. They are able to find spiritual values in everyday activities when they are connected to the cosmos. Recovering addicts experience, in a very real way, a *return of the spirit.*

All of the people that I have seen recover from the dis-ease of shame have had a spiritual transformation. All began their journey disconnected. Each found threads of connections that they built upon. Often these threads were discovered in 12-Step programs and deep process work.

Spirituality is often confused with religion. Unfortunately, religion can reflect the addictive system. Religions use control, dualism, and judgmentalism as means to achieve compliance. Religion is often a major source of shame for many individuals and groups. Spirituality is never a source of shame. Spirituality requires connection, and connection does not allow the shame experience. Transformation of shame involves a return of the spirit, a return to spirituality, and an acceptance of connections on all levels.

# CHAPTER 4

# SYSTEMS THAT PROMOTE SHAME

Although shame is an isolating experience, shame does not happen in isolation. Systems contribute to and reinforce the use of shame in an attempt to gain compliance of entire groups of people.

## Shame and Christianity

Shame is a vital component of Christianity. The Garden of Eden story makes clear that shame has been essential to control the behaviors of humans at least since the beginning of Biblical times. Missionaries have spent untold efforts persuading "heathens" around the world that shame opens the way to salvation through Christ, an outside source. Zealots have believed all those not following this sequence were doomed to damnation.

## Politics and Economics

Politics and economics, too, are strong proponents of

the use of shame to control behavior. To shame, to control, and to punish individuals, the English used a practice known as "sending one to Coventry" by which individuals were ostracized; no one spoke to such persons. This custom was transported to the United States and was used as a form of discipline in military schools as recently as the middle of the twentieth century.

Our economic and political system was built upon slave labor. Slavery has all the quintessential elements necessary in shaming. The goal of slavery is complete control over a group of people for the express purpose of financial gain of the controlling group. All of the elements used in shaming an individual can be recognized within the slavery system: abandonment, isolation, disassociation, blackouts, denial, terror, lying, judgmentalism paralysis, rage, spiritual crisis, self-centeredness, depression, fear of criticism.

The United States government used systemic shaming to help justify our encroachment onto Native American lands. Simple colloquialisms such as "Indian giver" form the ground work for countless other statements and attitudes aimed an controlling a large group of people who had something the U.S. government wanted.

## Education

Education often is a shaming experience for both children and adults. In many schools, controlling students, especially through shame, takes precedence over learning. Regularly, children are exposed as inadequate in one way or another. I still remember vividly the spelling bees held in my elementary school. I was almost always one of the first down, partly because I was a poor speller and partly because I so feared the shame of making a mistake I could not think to spell correctly. Such scenes are replayed countless times in a variety of ways in schools across the country and with remarkably similar results. Many children experience school as a hostile environment where their inadequacies are regularly exposed to the entire class.

In Western cultures, education has followed the model of the church, science, politics, and economics. It has become a segregating experience for most children. Children are separated from the rest of society in schools that segregate them even more by age, race, sex, intellectual ability, family income, religious affiliation, and other factors.

In my study of shame, I found the school system to be the second most prevalent source of shame for study participants. (Parents were the most often named source of shame.) Schools, by their structure and design, promote shame for virtually all students. Poor students are often shamed for doing poorly, but excellent students often feel shamed as well. The process of separating and judging students is a major factor in the development of shame.

Education appears to be one of the last bastions of pure mechanistic, reductivist thinking in the Western world. The world's information doubled between 1900 and 1950, and it is expected to have increased seven-fold between 1980 and 1990. This vast increase in how much information is available has had little impact on how education provides for learning. As our students' standardized college entrance scores go down, schools attempt to remedy the situation by applying more and more control to the education system, apparently oblivious to the inverse correlation between control and creativity and true learning.

## The Helping Professions

The so-called "helping professions," psychology and psychotherapy, also have supported the validity of shame. Few such practitioners question the legitimacy of shame per se; instead, they divide it into "good shame" and "bad shame." Many psychotherapists believe that "good shame," which arises from social taboos, keeps people from engaging in unacceptable behavior. Bad shame is that which has become so internalized that it emotionally cripples the person. Presently, a number of psychotherapists work with clients to reduce what the therapists deem "surplus shame."

Psychotherapy is usually thought of as a place to deal with an issue such as shame. Few have recognized that the process of psychotherapy often holographically mirrors the larger systematic reinforcement of the shame dynamic. In *Shame and the Search for Identity*, Helen Lynd stated,

> *Ruth Munroe reports that the aim of psychoanalysis is "fundamental change in the personality," to establish firmly "a basic shift in attitude." If this is true, then the psychoanalytic process would seem to have something in common with the substitution of one personality for another in military training ...and with religious and political conversion. The analyst, of course, always attempts to make the new identity that replaces the old what the patient "really" wants, just as the religious or political leader says that he is expressing the "real" wishes of the people.*

Lynd believes that social scientists have, for the most part, not questioned the difference between what is the norm and what is actually healthy for humans. This results in acceptance of *"the dominant values of the society as the norm of behavior, and to measure mental health and illness by them. Scientific objectivity, then, becomes indistinguishable from acceptance of social determinants."*

Traditional psychotherapy focuses on individual pathology. Sigmund Freud is the "father" of psychotherapy. For generations, his writings have influenced women's self-concepts, male-female relationships, and child-rearing practices. His explorations of the human psyche sought the origins of adult psychological problems in childhood behaviors and experiences. Yet, when he feared that the revelations of some of his patients might arouse the community against his work, he sacrificed the patients.

According to Alice Miller in *Banished Knowledge* and Jeffrey Masson in *Against Therapy*, personal documents recently discovered by Freud scholars indicate that under pressure from his medical peers and the elders of the community, Freud withdrew his initial report that some of his patients had been sexually abused as children. Instead, he reinterpreted as fantasies what the clients reported to him as recollections. Indeed, his writings contain long sections in which he "explains" the sexual fantasies of children.

Consequently, generations of psychotherapists followed his teachings and also refused to accept accounts of childhood sexual abuse as facts. As a result, the individuals experiencing the abuse were *worse* off. They were forced to think of themselves as such defective, incompetent, inadequate human beings that they didn't even know what really happened to them. Their shame was thus perpetuated and reinforced by the very people who should have been helping them. Freud's writings are one of the reasons that it took society so long to recognize the existence of childhood abuse and its long-term effects.

Recent research by D.B. Chamberlain shows that small children, even infants, are able to remember what has happened to them and to recall this information under certain circumstances. My work has given me the opportunity to witness clients recalling, through deep process work, events that occurred very early in their lives. These memories are not fantasies but, rather, valid recollections that have all too often insidiously damaged their lives.

## Science

Modern science also has promoted the use of shame. The basis of modern science is reducing things and ideas into their component parts in order to achieve control. This is called reductionism. Science has taught us that we can control almost anything, if we just break it down into its elementary parts.

The goal of modern science, that of control, has spread throughout Western cultures. Hence we now live with the illusion that control is the goal, not just of science but of life itself. We can see manifestations in the ways we talk to one another— "Get hold of yourself!"—and in the way we describe a person who cries— "He lost control." We fail to realize that people who express their feelings have not lost anything--in fact they have found themselves--by connecting to their feelings and allowing those feelings to be expressed.

### Systemic Denial, Individual Blame

Shame draws attention to the individual, but the shame of a larger system is often ignored. Shame is an isolating experience. Individuals and groups experiencing shame typically try to hide. The prevalent practice in psychotherapy is to focus on the individual and to ignore the larger system. For example, when a child is having problems in school, the child is usually blamed. Only in rare cases is the educational system questioned. The same process of blaming the individual or group occurs throughout our society. Yet it is usually the systems in which these people live that motivate the destructive behaviors and even encourage them. Our present economic, political and social systems tend to blame and shame people on welfare, yet the system does little to alleviate the problems causing economic poverty among large segments of society. Women face economic hardship when they get divorced, yet the laws continue to cause women and their children to join the ranks of the new poor, while their ex-husbands increase disposable income. The political system continues to protect powerful men while shaming and degrading women who might dare to speak up against them (Anita Hill is but one recent example). Entire groups of peoples are shamed through public policy in such actions as the "displacement" of Japanese-Americans during World War II and the appalling public policies that have served to attempt to eliminate Native Americans.

Helen, a woman I work with, reports, "During fifth grade, I used to play soccer in the school yard at lunch time. During one game I needed to urinate but I was reluctant to say so. Whenever I said, 'I need to go in,' Phil, the boy who was leading the game protested; he said I would break up the game. Finally my bladder gave up and the pool spread around my feet. I felt miserable and I think Phil felt equally bad. He saw it as his fault. No one blamed the social system that taught us that little girls must not let little boys know they need to go to the bathroom."

Denial occurs on a systemic as well as an individual level. Entire countries can deny what is happening. Post-World War II Germans denied any knowledge of what was happening to the Jewish people in concentration camps that were virtually in their backyards. People in other countries decried the German denial; yet, at the same time, other countries were involved in their own system-wide denial processes. The U.S. government released little or no information it had acquired on the existence and purpose of the camps.

Even after World War II, many Germans denied or hid their participation in the genocide policies of Hitler and the Nazis. Silence and denial permeated German culture for nearly 40 years. Only recently have their children and grandchildren begun to question what role their families had played and to face the shame of their parents' World War II activities.

While Germans were killing Jews in concentration camps, the United States and Canadian governments were "relocating" Japanese-American citizens. These Japanese-American citizens were detained in camps that were surrounded by barbed wire and under the guard of armed soldiers. They were precipitously deported from the West Coast where they had lost their jobs, their homes, their communities. Under the guise of national security, this entire group of people was separated from the rest of society because of their ancestry. For the most part, the larger society did not object: those that did object were faced with systemic shaming techniques.

The way we judge ourselves is a reflection of the judgmentalism practiced by society. Until recently, for example, society judged rape and sexual abuse as the fault of the victims. Also, our society, at different times has judged entire populations as inadequate— "less than." Economic, political, and educational practices systemically reinforce judgmentalism toward, for example, Native Americans, Blacks, Latinos, Asian-Americans, women, disabled people, etc. This systemic judgmentalism fosters systemic shame in these entire populations.

Another technique that supports the occurrence and perpetuation of shame is invisibility. It works in several ways. One way to control an individual or group is to treat them as if they do not exist, as if they are invisible. Women, people of color, lesbians, gays, and other minorities have had centuries of systemic experience with invisibility. Because they were held to be invisible, they did not count in governmental elections, legal determinations, politics, schools, or in the Church.

### Systemic Rage

Rage also is expressed systemically. Entire groups— even entire countries—can become caught up in rage. The scale covers incidents from local gang activities to tribal wars in Africa, Yugoslavia, and former members of the USSR, to international wars. Many people in the

United States still experience shame over our country's role in both the Vietnam War and the Persian Gulf War. In fact, in both hostilities, the systemic use of shame was a motivator as well as a diversion.

As a nation we have never fully acknowledged our motivation in or responsibility for the Vietnam War. Instead, we have done what shamed individuals often do: we have attempted to divert our shame by shaming the soldiers who did the fighting.

Young soldiers going to war in the 1960s for the most part believed that they were acting honorably. Many were stunned to return home to experience public shame, individually and as a group. Their trust in much of what the nation stood for was destroyed. The nation had changed while they were away and they became the brunt of our nation's rage. Consequently, many felt betrayed, duped, and shamed.

On a smaller scale, the opening in 1992 of a movie about African-American gangs, *Boyz' N the Hood,* was followed by seemingly wanton violence outside the movie theaters throughout the country. Young African-Americans faced with two hours of film portraying them as victims of society and of their own gangs left the movies and acted out their rage upon one another. In Minneapolis alone, one African-American teenager was killed and six other people were injured. Similar deaths and injuries occurred across the country.

In *The Addictive Organization,* Anne Wilson Schaef and Diane Fassel exposed the infrastructure—the addictive organization—that supports and reinforces the larger addictive system as well as the smaller systems: families, business, schools, religions, and individuals. The same is true for shame. The shaming process is used by addictive organizations to support and reinforce the larger addictive system—society itself—and the subordinate systems down to individuals as well. Replication occurs on all levels.

We can see the organizational process of shaming

throughout our society and our culture. The Catholic Church's response to clergy who have sexually abused children is a classic example of the shame dynamic. A priest in the midwest was reported to be involved in sexual abuse in numerous parishes for over a decade. Instead of dealing with his addiction, his superiors moved him from parish to parish and used the weight of the Church hierarchy to keep the victims quiet. When the abuse was finally brought to light by a young man who still suffered from the effects of being sexually abused as a boy, the Church reacted in a typical shame-based manner: first, its officials did not acknowledge their complicity but, instead, tried to hide the evidence of their involvement. Second, the officials were forced to admit their shameful conduct when they were compelled to provide evidence for the trial that confirmed the inadequacy of their behaviors. Third, the priest was made invisible yet again: he was whisked from public view, just as he had been from each individual parish where earlier complaints had arisen. Fourth, the priest became the target of the Church's rage. Under the guise of therapy, the priest was subjected to aversive therapy. He was required to look at pictures of young boys, and when he was sexually aroused, his genitals given a jolt of electric current.

Aversive therapy is a form of external control, of behavior modification. Like all other external controls, adverse therapy may cause more dysfunction than it cures. It changes nothing internally. The process the Church went through is similar to the process experienced by a family when it is faced with shame. Unless transformation occurs the system experiences isolation, disassociation, denial, exposed inadequacy, terror, lying, judgmentalism, breakdown of trust, rage, spiritual crisis, and the inability to process new information. The process of transformation is the same for individual, family and system: holographically, transformation in one area will affect all others.

The same sequence occurs in nonreligious organizations. A few years ago the director and founder of a nationally acclaimed children's theater company and school was charged with the sexual abuse of some male students. The school went through the same process the Church experienced. Many members of the school, faculty and employees and many parents and other people in the community had heard the rumor for many years that this man sexually abused children but no one did anything until a young man, who had been abused by the director, filed charges when he realized the director was abusing even younger boys. Then the accuser—the victim—was faced with isolation, disapproval, and anger by many parents and school-mates, not because he had been silent for so long but because he had exposed the director whom they looked up to!

The board of directors, all disavowed any knowledge of the director's sexual proclivities and took no responsibility for their silence or their implicit acceptance of the situation. In court, the evidence exposed the board to have been inadequate, just as the Church was found to be. The board's response was to make the director invisible. In a recently published history of the theater no mention was made of him although he had been the founder and the director for 16 years! He became the victim of a historical cover-up.

New rules were written forbidding teachers from entertaining students in their homes: an example of the belief that external controls can assure compliance. But again, nothing internal actually changed. Both the abusive director and complaining student disappeared from the scene. However, no one ever talked to the students directly about the situation. No one in positions of authority ever publicly admitted to her/his responsibility in the situation.

Treatment centers are often no better at dealing with systemic shame; indeed, they may actually practice it! In many centers, a client's denial is met with confrontation by staff members who verbally "beat" the client into submission. The group therapy "hot seat" often becomes a form of shaming sanctioned by the organization. The client, separated by the mechanics of the process, feels isolated while in the midst of the group. The client may feel tricked, judged, dumped on, and battered as the group, under the direction of the staff, exposes the person's inadequacy. This experience often becomes an excuse for staff members and other patients to vent their own shame and rage at the person in the hot seat.

Examples of techniques used by treatment centers to "break down" a client's denial are screaming, squirting her/him with a water gun, and "extinction" (acting as though the person did not exist, willing them into extinction). These are all components of the shame experience. All are attempts at control. The techniques are counterproductive in daily life but, perhaps, even more so in a treatment center where the goal is recovery from addiction. How tragic and ironic it is when treatment programs themselves operate addictively in the guise of curing addictions!

Going up a level to national shaming we see the same process at work under Nazis in Germany, with apartheid in South Africa, in our treatment of the soldiers who returned from Vietnam, in our response to opponents of the Persian Gulf War, and with how Native Americans, African Americans, Asian Americans, women, and other minorities are treated politically, economically, and socially in the United States. In each case the underlying processes of the shame experience are imposed upon entire groups of people. Our country is founded on the practice of using the various behaviors that induce shame to control vast numbers of people. Isolation, disassociation, denial, lying, judgmentalism, invisibility, self-centeredness, rage, and cutting off avenues of spiritual connections are the common techniques of control.

When our European forefathers wrote the Declaration of Independence, they began, *"We hold these truths to be self evident, that all men are created equal."* But at that time all men meant white men only. Excluded were all women, all children, and African, Native American, and other non-European men. All the excluded groups experienced systemic shaming techniques from the group in power. Although the most blatant forms have been discontinued, minority groups in the United States today continue to be shamed by social techniques on a regular basis.

One of the clearest examples of systemic shaming supported by the United States government was the nineteenth and twentieth century removal of Native American children from their parents and placing them in boarding schools. These boarding schools were only a part of a much larger process of separating Native American people from their culture, their spirituality, their identities, and nature. The schools often severely punished the Native American students who continued to practice their customs, language, and spirituality.

Phil Lane Jr., a Native American who has spent many years working with Native peoples throughout North and South America, stated, *"Little children entered the boarding school with a pure heart and left with a broken spirit."* Many Native Americans working in recovery see the residential schools as the root of Native American addictions. Lane stated, *"After the kinship ties were severed through generations of residential schools we became our own oppressors."*

The aftermath of boarding school education can be seen today in many cities and on many reservations. Native Americans have the highest alcoholism rate of any group in the United States. Their rate of graduation from high school is the lowest of any group in the country. A friend of mine, who has worked for many years with Native American youngsters who sniff noxious substances as a way to anesthetize themselves, cannot remember any sniffer who had not been a student at a boarding school.

Recovery from shame and from addiction must come from within. Transformation must emanate internally; it cannot be imposed. Recovering individuals know this on a personal level. It is just as true on a systemic level. Some Native American groups are attempting systemic recovery through an internal process by reclaiming their culture, their language, their dress, their spirituality in the schools they have organized. Piece by piece they appear to be taking back parts of themselves that were taken from them or that they had given away. They are reclaiming their power, not by blaming others but by recognizing and acknowledging their part in the loss. When a group faces responsibility for its behavior, it is able to move beyond shame; that is, it has transformed itself.

The Alkali Lake Band of Indians in British Columbia has accomplished such a transformation. In the early 1970's the entire population of the Alkali Lake Band was actively alcoholic. An internal transformation began when Phylls Chelsea, an Alkali Lake woman, decided to quit drinking and join AA. This transformation spread throughout the Band and 14 years later, 95% of the Band was sober. This transformation involved reconnection: with self, with a Higher Power, with other members of the band, with their children and with the larger community.

Holographic mirroring occurred on all levels. When the Native Americans oppressed themselves individually, they oppressed their families, their reservation community, the surrounding communities through their acting out while drinking. They were in the midst of performing a collective spiritual suicide. But when one person began to recover, the seeds were sown for the entire community to recover. A Honi Shori Elder stated,

> *We have to sit down and speak the truth to*
> *each other and make a peace among each*
> *other. That peace will bring unity and with*
> *unity there is strength and with the strength*
> *of unity we will have love and respect to walk*
> *in harmony with all life.*[2]

The members of the Alkali Lake Band, with the coopera-
tion of the Four World Development Project, are attempting
to heal themselves. In turn, they have begun to offer assistance to other indigenous groups wanting to recover from
alcoholism and transform the shame brought about by generations of systemic separation of children from their kin.

Phil Lane spoke these words when talking about their
recovery:

> *We free ourselves of the hurt and shame that*
> *binds us so that we can go on to the incredi-*
> *ble potentials and vision of the future. Until*
> *we cleanse our hearts and minds of the hurt*
> *we have gone through how can we see what*
> *true reality is all about? Its almost like we*
> *have some covering over the lens of our soul.*
> *So we must clean the mirror of our soul so*
> *that we can reflect the reality of the creator.*
> *The more we can reflect the divine reality the*
> *less need we have for things outside our-*
> *selves to give us happiness. We ourselves*
> *become a reflection of our creator's love.*

The Alkali Lake Band has done what Paulo Freire
talks about in *The Pedagogy of the Oppressed*. Each
member of the recovering community of Alkali Lake
Indians began with her/his own personal recovery. They
did not attempt to force others to join them, but through
persistent expressions of support and caring invited others to reconnect with them in sobriety. With sobriety
came a transformation of their shame, both individually

and as a community. Twenty years ago they were ridiculed and called the Indians of Alcohol Lake. Now they are a power world-wide.

As the Alkali Lake Indians have discovered, real transformation and recovery is never done in isolation. It always affects the wider community. The Alkali Lake Band has affected Native and non-Native peoples throughout the world.

Anthony Sutton in *Breaking Chains* discusses similar principles for descendants of slavery in the U.S. He offers a vision of an entire group of people crippled by what he calls "slave-shame" and then goes on to give concrete steps to transform "slave-shame."

Sutton sees "slave-shame" as a form of spiritual despair. This spiritual despair must be accepted, recognized, and dealt with for shame to be transformed. He sees recovery from shame following lines similar to those the Alkali Lake Band used so successfully.

# CHAPTER 5

# RECOVERY AND HEALING

Reconnection is essential for recovery from addiction; reconnection demands the individual's total participation in the process of healing. Reconnection brings with it a transformation of shame. The spirit returns. Shame evaporates when an individual or group is no longer isolated and recognizes the value of the self, which enables her/him to connect to other people and not to reject acceptance from them.

Through recovery many people have transcended the typical reactions to shame. Instead of isolation and hiding, they have discovered a new level of learning through facing their shame non judgmentally. The learnings from shame are vastly different for these individuals who have found a way to accept shame as a signal of something deeper. Invariably these people became active in a recovery program.

Recovery from shame involves, in the words of Paulo Freire, *"discovering themselves to be hosts of the oppressor."* Holographically, individuals and groups who experience shame will impose shame upon themselves and upon others. Individuals and groups in recovery from addiction and shame will not impose shame upon another.

All of the people whose stories have been told throughout this book experienced shame as debilitating. All needed to attain reconnection in order to heal shame. Reconnection usually began with telling a part of her/his life story. This procedure allowed the "teller" to begin to connect with her/his own story while listeners connected to both the "teller" and to parts of their own lives. Most of these people actively participated in ("worked") a 12-Step program as a part of their reconnecting to self, others, and a Higher Power. Through deep process work, each of the "tellers" reconnected with the feelings that often had been long denied, long distorted. Opening up to these feelings often was acutely painful initially but after the deep process work was completed some of the chronic, long standing pain was healed.

### 12-Step Programs

The 12-Steps—developed by Alcoholics Anonymous in the 1940s and now practiced by millions of people all over the world to recover from many addictions, not just alcoholism—offer a valuable, proven means of reconnecting. Used here with the kind permission of Alcoholics Anonymous World Services in New York, they read as follows:

1. *We admitted we were powerless over alcohol-that our lives had become unmanageable.*
2. *Came to believe that a Power greater than ourselves could restore us to sanity.*
3. *Made a decision to turn our will and our lives over the care of God as we under-*

*stood Him.*

4. *Made a searching and fearless moral inventory of ourselves.*

5. *Admitted to God, to ourselves and to another human being the exact nature of our wrongs.*

6. *Were entirely ready to have God remove all these defects of character.*

7. *Humbly asked Him to remove our short comings.*

8. *Made a list of all persons we had harmed, and became willing to make amends to them all.*

9. *Made direct amends to such people when ever possible, except when to do so would injure them or others.*

10. *Continued to take personal inventory and when we were wrong promptly admitted it.*

11. *Sought through prayer and meditation to improve our conscious contact with God as we understood Him, praying only for the knowledge of His will for us and the power to carry that out.*

12. *Having had a spiritual awakening as the result of these Steps, we tried to carry this message to others, and to practice these principles in all our affairs.*

For most people entering a 12-Step program, reconnecting is a terrifying prospect. However, the program allows each person to reconnect at her/his own speed. Some people attend meetings for months before they are able even to speak at a meeting. That is considered perfectly acceptable within this system. This *"loving acceptance of all members,"* as it is called in 12-Step programs, is part of the healing. This acceptance is an antidote to the years of judgmentalism.

The 12 Steps provide a framework in which to connect first with a Higher Power, then with self, and later with others. This sequence continues throughout the 12 Steps. Reconnection is the essence of all 12-Step programs. The 12 Steps provide a detailed, incremental means to accomplish this reconnection. The Second Step, *"Came to believe that a Power greater than ourselves could restore us to sanity,"* and the Third Step, *"Made a decision to turn our will and our lives over to the care of God as we understood God,"* both offer recovering people a context and a conduit for connection.

The Fourth Step of AA and other 12-Step programs offers a concrete way for many people to continue this process of reconnecting. It involves taking an inventory of one's strengths and weaknesses. An inventory is non-judgmental. It is merely an honest recognition of and listing of one's traits and characteristics. The process of recognition helps one to see the delusion and denial that are inherent in shame. The Fifth Step, *"Admitting to God, to ourselves, and to another human being the exact nature of our wrongs,"* involves exposing oneself to another person in addition to self and God.

Steps 6 through 11 continue the process of reconnecting to self, others, and a Higher Power. The Twelfth Step then guides the recovering person to externalize these internalized connections. It reads, *"Having had a spiritual awakening as the result of these Steps, we tried to carry this message to others, and to practice these principles in all our affairs."* When one can practice these connections in all her/his affairs, shame is transformed.

The 12-Steps are a powerful and necessary tool but, alone, are usually not sufficient for the transformation of shame. 12-Step programs provide a structure but not a means to re-experience long-denied feelings. For reconnection to occur, the individual must find an environment where it is safe to reconnect with these feelings. Reconnection involves much more then mere intellectual musings. It requires actual, full-body participation in the original experience without interference from outside sources. This environment is provided by Living in Process.

## Living In Process

Living in Process, a concept developed by author and facilitator Anne Wilson Schaef, is a systemic shift in the way people participate in the world. It requires the willingness to relinquish whatever gets in the way of personal knowledge and integrity. When one lives in process, there is no need to avoid or distort one's feelings. In other words, Living in Process is a paradigm shift out of the addictive process mode of operation into a mode that is based on honesty and the valuing of feelings as well as the intellect. Living in Process results in the elimination of delusion, denial, and dualistic thinking, the primary coping mechanisms in any addictive process. Addiction and its underlying shame are obstacles to Living in Process.

Living in Process is a cooperative journey. It aids those involved to follow the path toward reconnection with past feelings and experiences which were previously too painful and too terrifying to experience. The lack of judgmentalism in Living in Process often assists the person to reexperience the pain, but this time without the suffering inherent in judgmentalism. People who discover the freedom to feel the pain without the suffering are often eager to do work they had previously dreaded.

Most people living in Western cultures are so contaminated by the addictive process that they have no vision of Living in Process. Infants and small children naturally live in process. However, outside forces, parents and others, systematically work to eliminate this natural Living in Process by using shame and other techniques to control children.

To reconnect with one's own life in process, it is helpful to connect with other people who are attempting similar reconnections. Joining a group in which the participants honor and experience their own thoughts, feelings, and intuitions while, at the same time, challenging their delusions, denial, and addictions is valuable. Living in Process groups provide the nurturing environment.

Living in Process groups are typically conducted either through ongoing weekly or bi-weekly sessions or three to nine day "intensives." The participants in an intensive live together in a retreat setting without their usual everyday distractions. With both the ongoing groups and the intensives, the underlying process is the same. People come together with the expressed intent of attempting to live their lives as fully as they are capable of at the moment. This often involves taking risks of exposure of self to one's self and others. This exposure is accompanied with reconnection to self, others, the universe, and a Higher Power.

Living in Process groups are not therapy groups. Living in Process groups do not use psychological techniques and are not based on the illusion of control or scientific objectivity. In fact, Living in Process is the natural state of cultures that are not obsessed with controlling their members.

Groups are particularly helpful in allowing indiviuals to see other people experience strong feelings, "lose control," and thereby discover important information that has been previously unavailable to them person. Through membership in a Living in Process group, each individual is given the respect and consideration to observe, learn and participate at their own speed. For some this means quietly listening, without pressure from other members to perform in some preconceived way. For others it means beginning to notice when one's stomach begins to tighten, or when one's throat constricts, or when one's heart begins to pound. Each of these body changes, plus an infinite number of others can be a signal that the individual is ready to experience some feelings. Living in Process groups give the individuals an opportunity, if they wish to take it, to experience those feelings. Deep process work allows for the reconnection. It often begins with the sharing of issues with another person.

There is a 12-Step saying that *"You have to do the work yourself, you just don't have to do it alone."* Groups are a means of doing the work yourself in community with others on a similar path. Storytelling is vital in reconnecting with self, others, the universe and a Higher Power. Storytelling is an important part of Living in Process groups and by itself is not enough. Reliving old experiences and experiencing present feelings are also necessary for healing to occur.

Living in Process facilitation engages both facilitator and group member. The process involves the participation of the facilitator in her/his own life and in the willingness to be a witness to and participant in each group member's journey into her/his process. The participation includes sharing feelings, thoughts, memories, and plans. In addition, the participation involves "waiting with," rather than "waiting for," and it avoids any attempt to push or restrain the group member's own process.

When speaking, Schaef often describes the Living in Process facilitator as analogous to a midwife at a birth, whereas a therapist is like a doctor. A medical doctor may tire of waiting for the birth to occur naturally and use techniques (e.g., drugs, forceps, even surgery) to "control" the delivery. In contrast, the midwife's focus is upon "waiting with" the mother, assisting her as needed, yet staying in the background. To the midwife, birth is a process that involves the mother and infant; the midwife is there to assist and not to direct, control, or manipulate.

The Living in Process facilitator "waits with" a group

117

member. The facilitator does not presume to know where the group member is going in the process, therefore the facilitator does not attempt to control its direction or pace. What the facilitator does is simple but not easy in our control-driven world. The facilitator is truly present to the group member's experience: noticing and naming what is happening without judgment or attempts to manipulate. Living in Process facilitation is midwifery of the spirit.

Unlike psychotherapy, Living in Process facilitation uses no techniques, does not set up dualisms (right—wrong, good—bad, etc.), does not use interpretations, does not attempt to control, does not attempt to manipulate and does not use judgmentalism. The facilitator does not presume to know what is best or right for the individual or group.

Living in Process facilitators approach the people they work with as co-travelers on the road to recovery. In contrast, traditional psychotherapists present themselves as expert, objective observers and interpreters. They define the people they work with as clients or patients. The traditional psychotherapist approach of separation of self (expert) from client (object to be observed)[3] is in itself an act of shaming; it mirrors the disconnection inherent in shame holographically.

Living in Process facilitators first must do their own work. The facilitator must have faced and continue to face her/his own addiction, participate in her/his own recovery, and be willing to participate in another's recovery. Participation in another's recovery is vastly different from directing or controlling the other. Participation involves "responding with" rather than "reacting to." It involves faith in the universe and the holographic process of the universe that is not seen in psychotherapy. This faith means that the facilitator trusts that the group member has within herself/himself the knowledge necessary to live her/his own life. The facilitator does not pretend to be the "great imparter of knowledge," but is rather a witness to the other's redis-covery of her/his own truth, knowledge, and con-nections with self, others, and the universe. With this reconnection comes the transformation of shame. The transformation is from a disease of disconnection, a spiritual suicide, to the wholeness of reconnection.

## Beyond Treatment: Implications

*There is no transformation without recovery.*
- Diane Fassel
*There is no recovery without transformation.*
- Anne Wilson Schaef

Eastern philosophy teaches that the imposition of one's will upon another is, at a very fundamental level, an act of violence. Quantum physics echoes the same thought.

When Einstein was asked, "What is the most impor-tant question you have struggled with?" his answer was, *"Is the universe a friendly place?"* We still struggle with this question. Is it possible that the universe is friendly but that humans, in their use of modern science and their failure to respect the natural world, have made the it *un*friendly? Were the universe friendly, and were we to stop trying to control it, our lives would be radi-cally transformed. Examining the role of shame in the universe is part of the struggle against the illusion of control.

We are currently in the midst of a change in scientif-ic thinking. A new paradigm is in the making, one that is rejecting those aspects of modern science which are antithetical to the holistic view of the world. It is a dif-ficult process. In *The Aquarian Conspiracy*, Marilyn Ferguson wrote that *"Revolutions are not linear.... Revolutions shift into place suddenly, like the pattern of a kaleidoscope. They do not so much proceed as crys-*

*tallize."* Feminism, ecology, spirituality, and science, especially quantum physics and the science of chaos, are leading forces in this revolution.

Shaming does not work to control people. Shame initially may appear to control a specific behavior but often causes repercussions that are felt throughout the systems that have been long unrecognized. For eons, philosophers, social scientists, and theologians have believed that shame, used judiciously, could control unwanted tendencies in individuals. With recent developments in quantum physics, ecology, feminism, theology and other disciplines we are beginning to recognize that shame does not make a person a better member of society but, rather, promotes dysfunction individually and systemically.

As long as we refuse to allow individuals and groups to experience their feelings honestly we will distort or pollute feelings. This pollution may take many forms: addiction, shame, rage, etc. Only when we make a paradigm shift out of the mechanistic,[4] scientific, control-driven world view into one of connection and acceptance will feelings be viewed as gifts of connection to ourselves, to others, to a Higher Power, and to the cosmos.

Remembering that the world is holographic, if we wish to stop experiencing shame, we must simultaneously stop trying to control others by shaming *them*. As parents, we must reexamine virtually all of our child-rearing practices to see which of them foster, even demand, a shame response. As our illusion of control subsides, so do our attempts to make others conform to our ideas of who and how they should be.

By taking true ownership of *how I* feel and by staying with that as I decide what I will or will not do, I am much less likely to foster shame in another person. I have learned that when I am angry with another person, it is in my best interest — and theirs — for me to do my own "deep work" about it before confronting that person with my anger. When I do this, I am much less likely to "blast" another person or to say things that are hurtful and controlling — and much *more* likely to let the other person know how I am feeling and what *my* part in the situation is.

Schaef wrote in *The Addictive Society*,

> *The Addictive System is built on the process of the promise...and the promise of the Addictive System is that it is possible to have everything we want and need as long as we accept and conform to the system.*

This promise serves to control the behaviors of individuals and groups. It does not matter whether the promise is fulfilled as long as the individual or group somehow always can be blamed if things do not work out. Those who buy into the promise are always inadequate because they are incapable of achieving the promise. Thus the process of the promise serves to reinforce shame when the individual or group is blamed for the failure. It is only when individuals and groups begin to trust themselves as well as their feelings, impressions, and thoughts that they can begin to be a threat to the addictive system.

Recovery involves reconnections. AA and other 12-Step programs, in conjunction with Living in Process work, assist in making those reconnections. The reconnection to self involves recognition and acknowledgment not only of thoughts, but also of feelings, impressions, remembrances, and one's past. In Living in Process, the individual believes that he/she has the capacity and ability to work through a series of feelings without manipulation or control. When this occurs, the person discovers information previously unavailable to her/him consciously; often a new system emerges as a result. This new system takes the form of a different view of self, others, a Higher Power, and the cosmos.

Recovery work has shown that it is not so much a matter of what happened to a person, family, group, or society that determines the resultant dysfunction as it is the amount of denial, distortion, repression, and disconnection that ensued from the event. Reconnection, painful as it is, results in an acceptance of self. Acceptance of self results in transformation of shame.

We are at a critical point. There is no turning back. Addiction has become so ingrained in virtually all areas of our life that we are all contaminated by it. Shame is a part of this contamination. We can either continue to support addiction and the use of shame, or we can choose to face the shame and addiction in ourselves. Facing shame is an act of tremendous courage; it is a "leap of faith."

Learning is antithetical to the shame experience. When we face our shame, embrace it, feel it, then we learn from it. When shame is accepted, it is transformed. When we are connected to ourselves, to each other, and to the universe, we cease imposing our will on others. Shame is no longer needed. Spiritual suicide is no longer a viable option. Life, both physical and spiritual, becomes rich and full of meanings.

# NOTES

1 The fractal is a concept discovered by Mandelbrot. Fractals are numbers that are almost the same but not quite. He initially used fractals to plot the stock market, but quickly saw that fractals were useful in multiple areas such as the galaxies, blood circulation, and weather patterns. What Mandelbrot discovered in self-similarity was a repetition of detail at various sizes. He discovered that nature repeats and repeats itself at finer and finer levels of refinement. This new geometry leads to a confirmation of the world as a hologram. (Gleick, 1987).

2 Lucas, 1990.

3 Schaef, in press.

4 Belief that the world is a machine that can be taken apart and put back together again.

Alcoholics Anonymous. <u>Al-Anon's Twelve Steps and Twelve Traditions</u>. New York: Al-Anon Family Group Headquarters, 1985.

<u>Alcoholics Anonymous</u>. New York: Alcoholics Anonymous World Service, 1976.

Beattie, M. <u>Co-dependent No More</u>. Minneapolis: Hazelden Foundation, 1987.

Berman, M. <u>Coming to Our Senses</u>. New York: Bantam Books, 1989.

Berman, M. <u>The Reenchantment of the World</u>. Toronto: Bantam New Age Books, 1981.

<u>Bible: The New King James Version Containing the Old and New Testament</u>. Nashville: Thomas Nelson Publishers, 1982.

Black, C. <u>It Will Never Happen to Me!</u>. Denver: M.A.C. Publications, 1981.

Bohm, D. Postmodern Science and a Postmodern World. In D. Griffin (Ed.), <u>The Reenchantment of Science.</u> New York: State University of New York Press, 1988.

Bradshaw, J. <u>Healing the Shame that Binds You</u>. Deerfield Beach: Health Communication, Inc., 1988.

Chamberlain, D. B. The Outer Limits of Memory. <u>Noetic Science Review</u>. 1990, <u>16</u>, 4-13.

Eisler, R. <u>The Chalice and the Blade</u>. San Francisco: Harper San Francisco, 1987.

Elias, N. [<u>The History of Manners</u>]  (E. Jephcott, Ed. and trans.). New York: Pantheon Books, 1978.

English, H.B.& English, A.C. <u>A Comprehensive Dictionary of Psychological and Psychoanalytical Terms</u>. New York: David McKay, 1958.

Erikson, E. <u>Identity, Youth and Crisis</u>. New York: Norton, 1968.

Fassel, D. <u>Working Ourselves to Death</u>. San Francisco: Harper San Francisco, 1990.

Ferguson, M. <u>The Aquarian Conspiracy</u>. Los Angeles: Houghton Mifflin Company, 1980.

Fossum, M., & Mason, M. <u>Facing Shame</u>. New York: Norton Publishing, 1986.

Freire, P. <u>Pedagogy of the Oppressed</u>. New York: Continuum, 1988.

Freud, S. [<u>Civilization & its Discontents</u>] (J. Strachey, Ed. and trans.). New York: WW Norton, 1961. (Originally published, 1930).

Fox, M. <u>Original Blessing : a Primer in Creation Spirituality Presented in 4 Paths, 26 Themes and 2 Questions</u>. Santa Fe: Bear and Co, 1989.

Gleick, J. <u>Chaos: Making a New Science</u>. New York: Viking Press, 1987

Hartman, A. *Children in a Careless Society*. <u>Social Work</u>, 1990, <u>35,</u> (6), 483-484.

Hawthorne, N. <u>The Scarlet Letter</u>. New York: The New American Library of World Literature, 1959. (Originally published, 1850).

Kaufman, G. <u>Shame the Power of Caring</u>. Rochester: Books, 1985.

Koyre, A. <u>Galileo Studies</u>. Hassocks, England: Harvester Press, 1978.

Kuhn, T. <u>The Structure of Scientific Revolutions</u>. Chicago: University of Chicago, 1970.

Lewis, H. <u>Shame and Guilt in Neurosis.</u> New York: International

Universities Press, 1971.

Lewis, H. Shame and the Narcissistic Personality. In D. Nathanson. The Many Faces of Shame. New York: The Guilford Press, 1987.

Lucas, P. Healing the Hurt and Shame. Lethbridge, Alberta: University of Lethbridge, 1990.

Lucas, P. The Honour of All. Lethbridge, Alberta: University of Lethbridge, 1985.

Lynd, H. M. On Shame and the Search for Identity. New York: Harcourt, Brace and Company, 1958.

Mason, D. Shame is Losing Hold on Victims. Minneapolis Star Tribune, July 7, 1991, p. 17A.

Masson, J. M. Against Therapy. New York: Athenaeum, 1988.

Miller, A. Banished Knowledge. Doubleday: New York, 1990.

Miller, A. The Drama of the Gifted Child. New York: Basic Books, 1981.

Miller, A. Thou Shalt Not Be Aware: Society's Betrayal of the Child. New York: Meridian Books, 1984.

Nathanson, D. The Many Faces of Shame. New York: The Guilford Press, 1987.

Norberg-Hodge, H. Ancient Futures. San Francisco: Sierra Club Books, 1991.

Oxford English Dictionary (2nd ed.). Oxford: Clarendon Press, 1989.

Pearce, J. C. Magical Child. New York: Bantam Books, 1980.

Piercy, M. Woman on the Edge of Time. New York: Fawcett Crest, 1976.

Piers, G., & Singer, M. B. Shame and Guilt: a Psychoanalytic and Cultural Study. Springfield: Charles C. Thomas, 1953.

Polkinghorne, J. Science and Creation: The Search for Understanding. Boston: New Science Library, 1989.

Potter-Efron, R., and Potter-Efron, P. The Treatment of Shame and Guilt in Alcoholism Counseling. New York: Haworth Press, 1987. (c)

Potter-Efron, R. Shame, Guilt and Alcoholism. New York: Haworth Press, 1989.

Prigogine, I., and Stengers, I. Order Out of Chaos. New York: Bantam Books, 1984.

Ryan, W. Blaming the Victim. New York: Vintage Books, 1971.

Schaef, A. W. Beyond Science, Beyond Therapy. San Francisco: Harper San Francisco, 1993.

Schaef, A. W. Co-Dependency: Misunderstood/Mistreated. Minneapolis: Winston Press, 1986.

Schaef, A. W. Escape from Intimacy: Untangling the "Love Addictions:" Sex, Romance , Relationships. San Francisco: Harper San Francisco, 1989.

Schaef, A. W. Living in Process. San Francisco: Harper San Francisco, in press.

Schaef, A. W. Meditations for Women Who Do Too Much. San Francisco: Harper San Francisco, 1990.

Schaef, A. W. When Society Becomes an Addict. San Francisco: Harper San Francisco, 1987.

Schaef, A. W. Women's Reality. Minneapolis: Winston Press, 1981.

Schaef, A. W., & Fassel, D. The Addictive Organization. San Francisco: Harper San Francisco, 1988.

Sechrovsky, P. Born Guilty: Children of Nazi Families. New York: Basic Books, 1988.

Shiva, V. Staying Alive: Women, Ecology, and Development.

Atlantic Highlands: Zed Books, 1989.

Stevenson, B. McMillian Book of Proverbs, Maxims, and Famous Phrases. New York: McMillian, 1976.

Sutton, A.   Breaking Chains: Hope for Adult Children of Recovering Slaves. Minneapolis: Southside Pride, 1993.

Teilhard de Chardin.   The Phenomena of Man. New York: Harper Colophon Books, 1959.

Tomkins, S.   Shame. In D. Nathanson (Ed.).   The Many Faces of Shame. New York: The Guilford Press, 1987.

Twain,  M.   The Adventures of Huckleberry Finn. New York: Washington Square Press Book, 1963. (Originally published, 1884).

Webster, N. Websters New International Dictionary.   Revised J. McKechnie, Cleveland: The World Publishing Co., 1960.

Wegscheider-Cruse, S. Another Chance: Hope and Health for the Alcoholic Family. Palo Alto: Science & Behavior Books, 1981.

Wegscheider-Cruse, S.   Co-Dependence: An Illness, Describable and Treatable. St Paul: Nurturing Networks, 1984.

Wilber, K. (Ed.).   Quantum Questions. Boston: Shambhala, 1985.

Wilber, K. (Ed.).   The Holographic Paradigm and Other Paradoxes. Boulder: Shambhala Press, 1982.

Will, O. A., Jr.   The Sense of Shame in Psychosis:  Random Comments on Shame in the Psychotic Experience.  In D. Nathanson (Ed.), The Many Faces of Shame. New York: The Guilford Press, 1987.

Wurmser, L. The Mask of Shame.   Baltimore and London: Johns Hopkins University Press, 1981.

Zohar, D.   The Quantum Self. New York: Quill/William Morrow, 1990.

# ORDER FORM

# SHAME:
## *Spiritual Suicide*

by
**Vicki Underland-Rosow, Ph.D.**

**WATERFORD PUBLICATIONS**
**19835 WATERFORD PLACE**
**SHOREWOOD, MN 55331**
**PHONE 612-920-7511**

Please send_____ copy (copies) of ***SHAME: SPIRITUAL SUICIDE***

Please enclose $10.95 per copy.

**Sales Tax:**
Please add 6.5% for books shipped to Minnesota addresses.

**Shipping:**
Book Rate: $2.50 for first book and 75 cents for each additional book (Surface shipping may take three to four weeks)
Air Mail: $4.00 per book


Total enclosed $_____


Name_____


Address_____


City_____ State_____ Zip_____

# ORDER FORM

## SHAME:
### *Spiritual Suicide*

by
**Vicki Underland-Rosow, Ph.D.**

**WATERFORD PUBLICATIONS
19835 WATERFORD PLACE
SHOREWOOD, MN 55331
PHONE 612-920-7511**

Please send_____ copy (copies) of *SHAME: SPIRITUAL SUICIDE*

Please enclose $10.95 per copy.

**Sales Tax:**
Please add 6.5% for books shipped to Minnesota addresses.

**Shipping:**
Book Rate: $2.50 for first book and 75 cents for each additional book (Surface shipping may take three to four weeks)
Air Mail: $4.00 per book

Total enclosed $_____

Name_____

Address_____

City_____ State_____ Zip_____